TAPESTRY OF LIFE

Devotions
for The Unique Woman

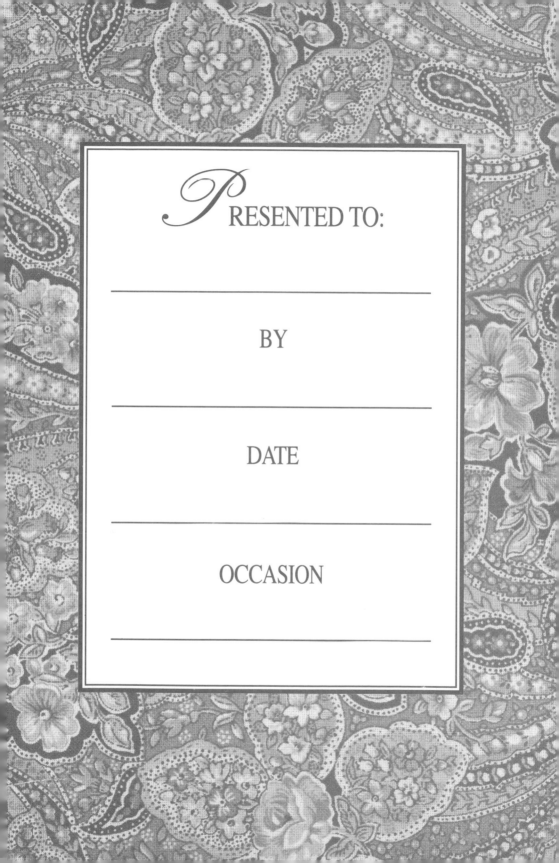

$\mathcal{P}$RESENTED TO:

_____

BY

_____

DATE

_____

OCCASION

_____

TAPESTRY OF LIFE

Devotions
for The Unique Woman

by
Nancy Corbett Cole

HONOR

Tulsa, Oklahoma

4th Printing
Over 76,000 in Print

Tapestry of Life —
Devotions for The Unique Woman
ISBN 1-56292-013-8
Copyright 1992 by Nancy Corbett Cole

Edwin Louis Cole Ministries
International Headquarters   West Coast Office
P. O. Box 610588   P. O. Box 626
Dallas, TX 75261   Corona del Mar, CA 92625

Published by Honor Books
P. O. Box 55388
Tulsa, Oklahoma 74155

CONTENTS

FOREWORD
by
Edwin Louis Cole

Anyone can know something, yet not do anything with the knowledge. To do something once is good, but excellence is being able to do it constantly. That is real "practice," consistently accomplishing the same thing. To live on a high level of consistency in obeying the Word of God, practicing a lifestyle that exudes excellence of spirit — that is true Christianity.

That describes Nancy, my wife.

This book contains a few of Nancy's introspective, reflective, meditative thoughts from a lifetime of Christian living. Scripture exhorts the more mature and experienced women to teach the younger,[1] and preparing this devotional for you is her way of obeying that injunction.

I have often said, fame can come in a moment, but greatness comes with longevity. Nancy has proven her greatness in her Christian life. She is a woman of integrity, courage and grace.

As you read her wise teaching, you will find comfort, wisdom, strength, understanding, truth, and most of all a profound and real love of God through the Lord Jesus Christ.

It is my delight and pleasure to indroduce to you the person I call "the loveliest lady in the land" — my wife, Nancy.

ACKNOWLEDGMENTS

I want to thank MarLynn Feuerstein, Belinda Sikes and our staff for their help. And to our editors, I say a big thank you for all their assistance in preparing this manuscript. I especially want to thank my daughter, Joann Cole Webster, for her hours of research and literary skills. Without her, none of this book would have been written. She has my deepest gratitude and admiration.

INTRODUCTION

Every woman takes the threads and materials each day hands her and works them into the tapestry that becomes her life. The quality of the materials handed to an ordinary woman will determine the quality of her tapestry. But the truly unique woman transcends inferior materials by spinning them through the hands of a loving Savior, Jesus Christ, and with His touch creates a tapestry that belies its raw beginnings — a tapestry that is truly beautiful and wondrously original. We can all become that kind of "unique woman" and find the Savior's pattern for our tapestry of life.

In this book, I write of real people's everyday events and emotions, and explore their inspiring responses. I believe with the action steps and scriptures to meditate on, you will find some strands of truth that will help you produce a richer, fuller life. Whether you read cover to cover, or simply as the need arises, you will find a new way to take life's common threads and, through the power of God, weave a portrait that is singularly your own — the beautiful creation God intended when He made you in your mother's womb — the masterpiece of His design, your unique tapestry of life.

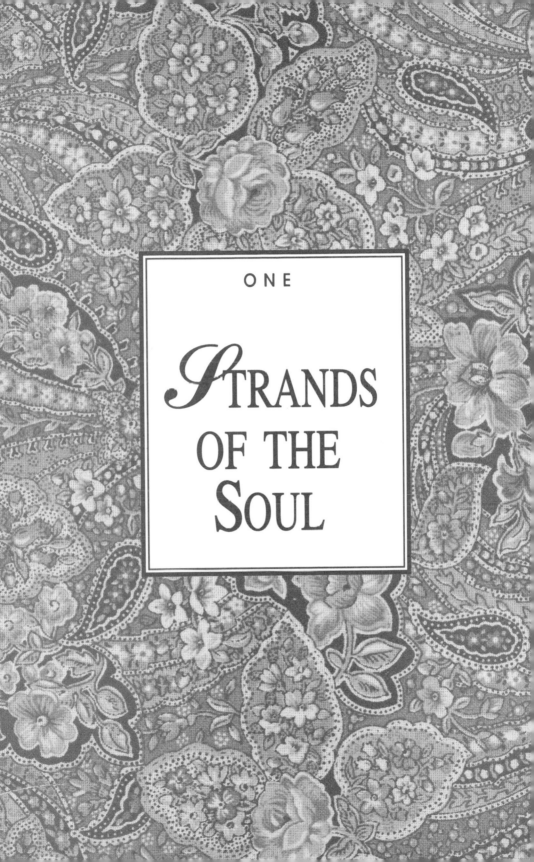

ONE

STRANDS
OF THE
SOUL

WISDOM:
Hope for Us All

Did you ever say, "That is the dumbest thing I ever did!" It probably isn't, but in the heat of the moment it feels as though it is. Perhaps you made an incredible blunder in the advice you gave someone.

Or did you ever "put your foot in your mouth," by saying the wrong thing at the wrong time? Some call it "Hoof and mouth disease." Those are the times when we wish the earth would suddenly open and swallow us up, or a flying saucer would suddenly alight and whisk us away forever.

Take heart — there is hope for you and all of us!

Not feeling very wise myself one day, I opened the Bible and there in Proverbs I read, "Does not wisdom cry out? and understanding put forth her voice?"[1] It seemed as though I had never read it before. I always begged and pleaded God for wisdom, but God tells us wisdom is right there, whenever we need it.

This gives us wonderful hope, because another Proverb says that even a fool seems to be wise if he doesn't open his mouth.[2] I can't always spout wisdom when called upon, but I can honestly tell someone, "I don't have the answer but I will certainly pray about it. Perhaps God will give you the answer or He might give it to me." At the very least, our hearts are knit together to wait for God's answer.

There is a lot more involved than just praying, because we have to pray in faith, and according to the will of God.[3] Depending on our age, there are not going to be six lollipops on our pillow in the morning, or three Rolls Royces in the front driveway. That is not how God answers prayer. But He does answer. So if we ask for wisdom, He is going to give it. It may be gradual, something that comes as we grow in Him, or we may have a burst of wisdom as the need arises. Let God do it in your life!

ACTION STEPS

* To gain wisdom, you have to know the Word of God. Edwin and I have a practice of reading a chapter in Proverbs every day. Since there are thirty-one chapters, we finish the book every month. Memorize James 1:5 and make it your own!
* Be very conscious that God is patiently waiting to give you wisdom, when you are in the place to receive it.
* In your daily Bible reading, take one verse to meditate on all day long. Meditation goes a long way in gaining wisdom.

WORTH QUOTING:

"Fill your house with the Word, and the house will fill up with riches and wealth."
— *Marilyn Hickey*[4]

"Authority without wisdom is like a heavy axe without an edge, fitter to bruise than polish."

— *Anne Bradstreet*[5]
(1612-1672)

UNDERSTANDING:
Now I Get It!

The Proverb says that when we ask for wisdom we need to get understanding, too.[1] We do not always understand every situation. When we know only a part of the story we can be overly pessimistic or optimistic.

A friend named Sharon became angry at her father for not paying attention to her when she was growing up. He never hugged her, much less kissed her on the cheek. When Sharon learned as an adult how a good father treats his children, her attitude toward her father hardened. Though he had never abused her, she felt emotionally neglected.

One day at a family gathering, a relative told her some things about her father's childhood. His mother died when he was a young boy, and one day when he came home from school, his family had moved! No one had bothered to tell him. Someone eventually came for him, but his was a household with no communication, little love shown, no touching, and the children did not learn much about parenting.

Sharon finally understood. She immediately forgave her father for the things he did not know. The love she had for him as a child came rushing back. She began to remember how her father denied himself material comforts for the sake of his family, how he provided for them, and was always there, even if buried in a newspaper. Sharon recognized her father's love that he simply never could express.

Often the differences we experience with others are based on a lack of understanding. Do you know someone who is friendly one day and cold the next? We do not know their anguish and pain. Thousands of people have come from neglectful and abusive pasts. We need understanding!

Is your husband morose, short tempered, not his usual self? Perhaps something upset him, or he is in an internal crisis.

Perhaps just a warm hug or the words, ''I love and appreciate you,'' is all someone needs to hear from you.

It's the same with children. When children grow into adults, they tell parents of adventures and incidents from their childhood that the parents were completely unaware of. We often think of children as being carefree and happy. But a child's world is much more limited than ours, so when calamity befalls them, such as being embarassed, that child's pain is excruciating. This is also true when we surround them with negative comments such as, ''You're just like Uncle Ned'' (Uncle Ned being the relative nobody likes). We need understanding!

We need understanding in every aspect of our lives and with every one we come in contact with.

ACTION STEPS

* Have you been the victim of misunderstandings? Forgive those involved, and let the incident become your motivation to keep from misunderstanding others.
* If you err, err on the side of love. I can't remember who first spoke these words to me, but they have been valid for a lifetime. It is better for all concerned to give someone the benefit of the doubt than to write them off.
* If someone in your life is particularly difficult, try to research a little about his or her past. A little light shed can produce a lot of understanding.
* Do you feel like you would like some encouragement, someone to hug you and appreciate you? If you are bold enough, and have friends close enough, ask for it! Otherwise, go find someone whom you can do this for. It is very rewarding to give to others what you wish to have yourself. ''Give, and it shall be given unto you.''[2]

WORTH QUOTING:
''Few, save the poor, feel for the poor.''
— *Letitia Elizabeth Landon*[3]
(1802-1838)

FORGOTTEN:
God Never Forgets

God never forgets us! Yesterday Edwin called me from a distant city, but for hours before his call I thought he had forgotten. That *forgotten* feeling is one of the worst I know.

A friend who today is an internationally renowned Bible teacher grew up in a country where her Christian denomination did not allow women to teach in church. She loved God and spent hours alone with Him in prayer and Bible study. Whenever God gave her insight, she taught it to other women. As she continued steadfastly studying God's Word and relaying it to women, God poured His wisdom into her and gave her a desire to teach the whole Body of Christ.

Years stretched out as she waited for the Lord to fulfill this desire. Almost a full decade later, God suddenly told her during prayer, "I want you to take this message to the United States." Stepping out by faith with the agreement and support of her husband, she went. She knew few people when she arrived in the U.S., but after one church engagement, news quickly spread that this was a woman under the hand of God. After a few more engagements, she became busy night and day teaching profound truths that were new to us. Her ministry path crossed mine and Edwin's at that time and her teaching had a remarkable impact on our lives.

She gained my immediate respect when I heard how for years she never gave up waiting on God! We cannot allow ourselves for one minute to think God has forgotten us or His promises to us. *God never forgets!* You can trust that God remembers you every minute and knows where you are right now.

ACTION STEPS
- Write down the promises God has made to you. Write the date that fulfilled ones came true. Encourage yourself with all the promises that were fulfilled.

* Look up God's promises for His people in the Bible. Those were made with you in mind! Write them out and read one or more aloud during your private prayer time.
* Concerning things you believe God wants you to do: Start where you are with what you have. Don't wait until you think you are perfectly ready or timing is perfectly right. The Bible says that if you wait for perfect conditions, you will never get anything done.[1]

MEDITATION:

"How precious it is, Lord, to realize that you are thinking about me constantly! I can't even count how many times a day your thoughts turn towards me. And when I waken in the morning, you are still thinking of me!"

— Psalm 139:17,18 TLB

IMAGINATIONS:
Willy-Nilly Feelings

Imagination is funny at times, actually strange. We can get worked up about almost anything, often to find it was just a puff of air. I remember as a child I vividly pictured my parents dying and leaving me an orphan. I cried so hard that my mother thought I was sick and put me to bed. I was too embarrassed to tell her the real problem!

Mary was a friend of mine who lived in agony for weeks because when her husband went out walking, he always talked to the pretty neighbor next door. Thinking he was having an affair, Mary could think about nothing else and cried out to the Lord daily. She finally wore herself out and, at her regular prayer time, could not even continue to pray. It was then that she sensed the Holy Spirit urging her to return to reality and see what her husband did when he walked. She mustered the courage to go with him the next day and discovered that he talked to all the neighbors, not just the one woman. She asked him about it and found out that he liked the neighborliness he felt when he made friends in the community.

She was so relieved and chagrined that she didn't admit her foolishness to anyone for years, but appreciated and loved her husband more than ever.

The Bible tells us to bring every thought into captivity,[1] disciplining our minds so they do not go on a wild rampage. God's perfect love casts out all fear,[2] and replaces the fear that leads us on such wild rampages, as we meditate on Him and His Word. A song lyric states, "Imagination is silly, you go around willy-nilly."[3] Let's not be willy-nilly Christians!

ACTION STEPS
* Do you have a "wild imagination" that crops up? Usually, there is a pattern — always negative about a certain situation, or always positive along the lines of fantasy. Capture those wild thoughts! Ask the Lord to take care of the issues in your life that lead you

to think in those patterns. As you deal with issues, not false imaginations, you will see real answers to prayer!

• In your prayer time, train your thoughts on the Lord, not on stray thoughts that rob you of your time with Him. When you have legitimate thoughts you don't want to forget, have a pen and paper handy to jot those things down, then get right back into prayer. You have scheduled the time in the midst of your busy life, now guard that time!

LET'S PRAY:

Father, help me to cast down every imagination — every thought that is not profitable for me to hold onto. In the name of Jesus, keep me from letting my thoughts wander; help me to train my thoughts according to Your Word. In Jesus' name I pray. Amen.

MEDITATION:

''These weapons can break down every proud argument against God and every wall that can be built to keep men from finding him. With these weapons I can capture rebels and bring them back to God, and change them into men whose hearts' desire is obedience to Christ.''

— 2 Corinthians 10:5 TLB

FAITH:
Or Was That Fantasy?

If I recommended that everyone buy a plaid couch, I would get both love and hate mail, because what is great for one person's living room is an eyesore for another. Distinguishing between faith and fantasy is equally difficult because what is faith for one person might be fantasy, mistaken for faith, by another. Faith is rewarded by God and releases His power. Fantasy is unfulfilling, and hinders God's power.

I received a letter from a desperate woman who felt she would die if God didn't restore her marriage. Then she explained that her husband had been gone several years and had three children with a new wife. Though I hurt for her, I suspected she was led more by fantasy than faith.

Many single women nurture emotional ties, thinking to perform a super-spiritual act of courage by believing — with no basis in fact — that God has revealed their husband to them. Other women fantasize of some great thing happening.

My mother-in-law prayed for her husband's salvation and received God's assurance of it. Mom is a powerful woman of faith, but as she pressed on in prayer year after year, she began to dream of a wonderful ministry they would have once he was saved. Instead, just two days before his premature death, he gave his heart to the Lord. Mom was deeply disappointed.

She was gardening shortly after the funeral, working through her grief. Hunched over a flower bed, she stabbed at the dark earth and cried bitterly, "God . . . I thought we were going to have a great ministry! I thought . . . . "

God suddenly, with sweet firmness, spoke to her spirit: "I promised to save him. You added the rest."

Mom sat back on her heels, instantly perceiving her blindness to the joy of His fulfilled promise. Her husband was saved and rejoicing in heaven at that very moment! With a new, heavenly perspective, she lifted her head, raised her gloved hands and, looking into the bright sunlight, she began to shout, "Hallelujah! Praise be to the Lord!"

Mom learned a lesson we all need to learn. We tend to fantasize about what our children will become, or how we'll act when we win an award, all the while allowing fantasy to rob us of the joy of true faith — seeing God answer our prayers according to His will. God will not honor fantasy, but He does honor faith.

ACTION STEPS

* It's pretty hard to get carried away with fantasy when we pray the Word of God. Find scriptures that pertain to your specific need, and bring those to the Lord in prayer. Discipline yourself to pray only as He leads, not from your own ideas.
* Is there a person you need to release from your own fantasies? Yourself, your child, husband, or future husband? Take your inventions and fantasies to the Lord in prayer. Don't be embarrassed, because He already knows what they are and loves you anyway. Tell Him your fantasies, repent for vain "imaginations,"[1] then ask Him to replace the fantasies with His Word, so you can meditate on it both "day and night."[2]
* When we pray for people's salvation, it is important simply to ask God to save them, not invent some monumental work these people will do once saved. First things first! Let's let them become saved, grounded in the Word, and full of the Holy Spirit before we make them superheroes!

LET'S PRAY:

"Father, You know my heart and the guilt I have brought on myself. I confess my fantasies to You right now and ask You to cleanse me from this unrighteousness according to Your Word. I release everyone involved in my fantasy world to be the people You made them to be. Give me new eyes, I pray, to see them as You see them — as they really are. Please help me replace my fantasies with meditation on Your Word so that faith will grow in my heart. I ask this in the name of Your precious Son, Jesus. Amen.

MEDITATIONS:

"So then faith cometh by hearing, and hearing by the Word of God."
— Romans 10:17

"But his [a Christian's] delight is in the law of the Lord; and in his law doth he meditate day and night. And he shall be like a tree planted by the rivers of water, that bringeth forth his fruit in his season; his leaf also shall not wither; and whatsoever he doeth shall prosper."
— Psalm 1:2,3

"Now faith is the substance of things hoped for, the evidence of things not seen."
— Hebrews 11:1

BITTERNESS:
From Gloom to Glow

How would you feel if you were a faithful, church-going wife and mother and one day found out your husband was addicted to pornography — in fact had a whole basement full of it? When this happened to my friend, Marie, she resisted every temptation to become bitter, and turned her full attention to the Lord.

Marie and Bob had many marital problems, so the pornography simply "iced the cake." But she believed God could deliver Bob from this powerful addiction and restore their marriage. Marie overcame her feelings of disgust by earnestly praying for him. When she heard of a church meeting for men in their city, she urged Bob to go and he agreed. During the message, the preacher asked for men who had lust in their hearts to come to the altar for prayer. Bob went forward, and returned home to throw out the pornography. But within weeks he bought more. Marie was heartsick, but undaunted in prayer and faith.

At Marie's urging, Bob went to another meeting in another city with the same speaker. Again, he went forward for prayer. Again, he did not feel as though he could shake the addiction that ruled his life. He went home, threw away the pornography, but returned to it within weeks. Marie persevered in prayer. Bob went a third time to yet another city to hear the speaker again, and this time he was completely delivered from the disabling addiction that was destroying his family.

After his spiritual breakthrough, he began to tell everyone about Jesus. He found a "captive" audience in the local prisons and became an ordained prison chaplain. Through perseverance and prayer, Marie has watched her husband change from a rough, tough pornographer to a humble, loving minister.

Marie also is a new woman and their marriage is completely healed. She could have wallowed in self-pity, resentment and bitterness but instead took the positive approach and believed in a powerful God. She is so happy, her countenance has changed from one of gloom to a healthy glow.

ACTION STEPS

* Who have you "written off" as being beyond hope for salvation? No one is beyond the great arm of God — thankfully! Turn that list of "write offs" into a prayer list and see what God does without you ever saying a word, except to Him.

* Where are the bitter areas of your life? Toward whom, or what, are you embittered? Clyde Besson, a Christian minister and author, teaches an exercise which he calls a "Bitterness List." Find a secluded place to spend an hour (perhaps locked in your bedroom or bathroom?). Take a piece of paper and put one person's name at the top. (Make a separate list for each person.) On the left side, list what they did and on the right side, list how it made you feel. Now take a red pen and begin to mark through those feelings as you cover them with the blood of Jesus in prayer. Release all "rights" to anger and hurt as you accept Jesus' provision on the cross to heal you of all those hurts. Now start down the other side of the list, forgiving the person for those offenses, crossing them out with the red pen symbolizing the blood of Jesus that forgives us of all our sin. When you are finished, say out loud, "This is covered with the blood of Jesus, never to be remembered against me or this person again." Then destroy it! We have precious few years on this earth with precious little love to glean, and no time or emotion to waste on bitterness!

QUOTABLE QUOTES:

"I realize that patriotism is not enough. I must have no hatred or bitterness towards anyone."

> — *Edith Cavell,*[1]
> *before being unjustly executed*
> *(1865-1915)*

ATTITUDES:
Will and Determination

Our attitude about any situation is our choice. We can will ourselves to love or hate, yell or laugh, hold a grudge or forgive. This is why God can command us to forgive, to love, to overlook an offense. But God not only requires a positive attitude, He enables us to have one. As we willingly yield to Him, and His Spirit fills our lives, our attitudes naturally change.

At a friend's home Bible study last month, I met Janet, a thin, angry young woman in a leather jacket. She attended out of loyalty to our host, a mutual friend, but that night Janet recognized her need of Jesus and received Him as Savior. The next week she looked inexplicably different. In the few weeks since then, her attitude has completely changed.

She reminds me of some women I knew years ago. I knew them only as Puritan-looking spinster ministers in the mountains of Northern California. I assumed they had never seen a television or worn make-up and simply lived in complete devotion to the Lord. Years later I learned that they had been Harley-Davidson-riding, leather-clad, hardened drug users in the San Francisco area who attended a revival meeting and were gloriously converted. Talk about a change of attitude!

But what do we make of those who have known Christ, yet still maintain a poor attitude? I believe they are simply unwilling to yield to that attitude-changing Spirit within them. I know a woman who has to travel, but hates it. Because of a poor attitude, she feels every inconvenience — all the rushing, waiting, and pushing. I also know a man who dislikes business travel but decided to take up genealogy. Everywhere he goes, he calls people with his surname from local telephone directories. He has discovered almost every branch of his ancestry and collected enough family data to write a book! What if my woman friend decided to find things she likes, too? Studying local history, visiting art museums, investigating regional foods, reading without interruption or studying the Bible in-depth could be a great blessing by an act of her will.

A poem I read once said, "I lamented the fact that I didn't have new shoes, until I met someone with no feet." Your attitude is your choice!

ACTION STEPS
- The Apostle Paul was persecuted, beaten, imprisoned and in need of food and clothing, but he wrote, "I have learned to be content in whatever circumstances I am."[1] In what areas of your life is this *not* your attitude? Find things, however small, that do please you, and begin building a new attitude from it. "Godliness with contentment is great gain."[2]
- Is there a particular person toward whom you have a negative attitude? Perhaps your supervisor at work is overbearing. Or someone in the church is always sticking his or her nose in everyone's business. Begin to pray earnestly for that person. Prayer changes things. You will begin to grow in love for the one you are praying for, and your attitude will change from intolerance to compassionate concern.
- Is there a particular part of your life that is extremely stressful or discomfiting? Perhaps it is not you, but your husband who travels and you can hardly stand to have him go (or come back?)! Take control of yourself in those situations! Spend some time thinking of the attitudes of every person involved. Is everyone having an equally hard time? What can you do to help? Pray about changing your attitude. God will work miracles when just one person humbles himself or herself and begins to do the right thing — starting with prayer! It is your choice.

THINK ABOUT IT:
" . . . whatever is true, whatever is noble, whatever is right, whatever is pure, whatever is lovely, whatever is admirable — if anything is excellent or praiseworthy — think about such things."
— Philippians 4:8 NIV

"I am not saying this because I am in need, for I have learned to be *content* whatever the circumstances."
— Philippians 4:11 NIV

PICTURE THIS:
One day a lady criticized D. L. Moody for his methods of evangelism in attempting to win people to the Lord.

Moody's reply was, "I agree with you. I don't like the way I do it either. Tell me, how do you do it?"

The lady replied, "I don't do it." Moody retorted, "Then I like my way of doing it better than your way of not doing it."[3]

WORTH QUOTING:

"Whoever is happy will make others happy too. He who has courage and faith will never perish in misery!"

— *Anne Frank*[4]
(1929-1945)

" 'tis the set of sails and not the gales which tells us the way to go."
— *Ella Wheeler Wilcox*[5]
(1850-1919)

"Beauty is in the eye of the beholder."

— *Margaret Wolfe Hungerford*[6]
(1855-1897)

FAITHFULNESS:
Count On Me

We often think of faithfulness in the context of marriage. Without faithfulness, no one can have a solid marriage with trust and commitment as its corner-stones. But there is a lot more to faithfulness than that.

The dictionary defines *faithfulness* as: unswerving devotion, loyalty to one's promises, trustworthiness. The Bible says, "A faithful man who can find?"[1] and, "The Lord preserves the faithful."[2]

Edwin and I went to pastor a fairly large church where an older woman attended whose arms and hands were crippled with arthritis. This sweet woman always sat in the same place and never missed a service. I was very surprised to learn that she was the one who faithfully prepared every communion service. Forgetting her disability, with great physical strain and pain, she performed what was truly a "labor of love."

Faithfulness is a sterling quality. Successful businesses always operate by faithfulness. Our postman is faithful, delivering our mail daily. And we would be shocked if our grocery store were closed on a day when it should be open. Our children even learn this, for school starts and stops on time, and children are recorded if they are one minute late.

Successful people are also faithful. Whether able-bodied or not, the people who we really trust are the faithful, the "doers." Once they have a task and understand how to complete it, we never think of it again except to say "thank you" when it's done.

We need to work at being faithful for not only is it the mark of the successful, but it is also the mark of the godly. God is faithful. We plant a seed in the ground, water it, feed it, and know it will grow based on the laws of nature that God has laid out.

Have you ever said, "I'll do it," only to disappoint those you promised when you don't do it? We are unfaithful sometimes to our children. We give reasons for not following through, but the fact remains, we weren't faithful.

We need to work on being faithful to God and people. What a reputation to have, for our children, husband, or friends to say, "You can always count on her to keep her word."

ACTION STEPS

• Have you given your word to someone and never apologized when you did not follow through? However late, the apology is always welcome, and it will clear your conscience as well.

• Do you have a problem saying "no" to people, even when you know you cannot possibly do what they have asked? Practice! Have a friend ask you to do difficult assignments and make a game of saying "no." Learn how to be polite but firm, then start saying "no" first until you get yourself out of the habit of "yessing" everything. You can always go back and volunteer to help if you believe God wants you to.

• Are you afraid to get involved in anything for fear you will not complete it? Learn to be faithful in the small things first. Promise something to yourself or others that is easy to accomplish, then slowly work up to the more difficult tasks.

FOOD FOR THOUGHT:

"Doing the Father's will is for Christ the essence of obedience, not merely conformity to an external code."

— Susan Muto[3]

WORTH QUOTING:

"Merely to obey rules at a superficial level and not to allow God total access to our person prevents us from having deep contact with God."

— *Rebecca Manly Pippert*[4]

"Scheduled withdrawing to God is what will establish, strengthen, settle you in the disciplines of your heart."

— *Anne Ortlund*[5]

ANGER:
Emotion or Sin?

Anger is an emotion that most of us try to keep in check. But sometimes we are overwhelmed and lose our temper.

A friend of mine was shocked one day when she reached out angrily and hit her teenage son. Even though she was a child of God, she lashed out in a way totally contrary to the Christian life. For this reason, the Bible says to "grow" in the Lord.[1] The "fruit of the Spirit"[2] such as joy, peace and patience are not instantly part of our lives the moment we accept Jesus Christ as our Lord and Savior. Instead, we must painstakingly give our old lives over to the Lord, slowly but surely committing ourselves to Him and becoming alive to His regenerating Spirit in each area of life.

As my friend meditated on her behavior, in light of God's Word, she realized that she had some deep resentments. In prayer, she asked forgiveness, forgave others, and cleansed her heart. Then she apologized to her son, and rightly so. When we apologize to our children for bursts of anger, we let them know that angry explosions are not acceptable even for us, and we expect him or her to follow our example.

The Bible says that explosions of anger are sinful, but anger in itself is simply an emotion, not a sin. Jesus certainly did not sin when he was angry with the Pharisees. Anger can be used in a positive way as a motivation to pray, protect or persevere. But when anger just simmers in the heart unchecked, it can produce depression and angry outbursts. As we give anger an outlet through prayer in our private time with the Lord, we give God the opportunity to use it as motivation in our lives, and we give ourselves the opportunity to grow in the fruit of the Spirit.

ACTION STEPS

* Much of popular psychology involves dredging up old memories in order to vent anger. But the Bible says it is foolish to stir up anger.[3] This means that purposely trying to bring up old memories in order to make ourselves angry is in some way foolish. I believe

this is because we are often not ready spiritually for God to deal with such things. Instead of dredging, the Bible gives numerous illustrations of clearing our hearts by meditating on the Lord, not our pasts, and giving Him permission to bring up whatever He wants. When God brings up the old hurts and injustices, we can trust Him to finish what He starts!

- Prayerlessness is a form of hiding. If you don't want to pray, you may really be trying to hide something deep within. Be courageous! Nothing that comes up can overcome you! God will give you the ability to face your deepest fears, and conquer them. Yield yourself to Him and He will do the work. A good, solid, praying Christian counselor can help.
- Deep breathing helps in tense situations. Oxygen released to the brain actually enables us to think more clearly and respond with more forethought instead of exploding. Try taking a deep breath the next time you are tempted to blow — or take several!

MEDITATIONS:
"And be ye kind one to another, tenderhearted, forgiving one another, even as God for Christ's sake hath forgiven you."
— Ephesians 4:32

"A wrathful man stirreth up strife: but he that is slow to anger appeaseth strife."
— Proverbs 15:18

"Surely the churning of milk bringeth forth butter, and the wringing of the nose bringeth forth blood: so the forcing of wrath bringeth forth strife."
— Proverbs 30:33

THINK ABOUT IT:
"Be not hasty in thy spirit to be angry: for anger resteth in the bosom of fools."
— Ecclesiastes 7:9

SELF-IMAGE:
God's Image of Us

"Self-image" simply stated is how you perceive yourself in your innermost being. If you feel accepted and you mutually respect people, you are said to have a "healthy self-image." Without that, feelings of inadequacy envelop your life resulting in a "poor self-image."

I greatly admire Eleanor Roosevelt for changing from a poor to a healthy self-image in her adult years. She felt she had to do something when her husband, who happened to be President of the United States, became ill. When she accepted some invitations to speak, a friend cautioned, "Speak slowly and sit down when you have nothing more to say." Understanding just those two rules, she spoke and was remarkably well-received. Soon, instead of thinking she should stay in her husband's shadow, she became confident she had something to offer and strode into public service.

My daughter, Lois, learned new confidence as a prosecuting attorney. Naturally shy, she approaches many jury trials thinking of her inadequacies. One day she was attempting to convict a man of sexual child abuse. Listening to the lies of the defendant and his counsel, she became so enraged that she fired off an eloquent closing argument. When the jury returned with a guilty verdict, the man's defense attorney commended her, saying, "That was the most convincing argument I have ever seen you give." Why?

Because she forgot herself and swallowed up her own inadequacies to protect a little girl.

Insecurity and shyness are fed by thinking more about ourselves than the people we are with. Try forgetting yourself and concentrate on that other person!

Authority figures may have criticized you with remarks like "You're big/athletic/loud for a girl!" Critical remarks keep many of us from joining the mainstream. Insecure women may feel as if they are at the mercy of other people in life. Starved for recognition, they may call attention to themselves by bragging or complaining.

The Psalmist declared, "How precious it is, Lord, to realize that you are thinking about me constantly! I can't even count how many times a day your thoughts turn toward me. And when I waken in the morning you are still thinking of me!''[1] What recognition! The Bible says we are the daughters of God and joint-heirs with Jesus Christ.[2] Meditating on such verses helps bolster self-confidence, and rids us of self-deprecation and defeatism.

Lose sight of yourself, and become identified with the person God says you are. As we believe His perspective of us, we gain the greatest self-image possible.

ACTION STEPS
* The saying goes, ''Let go and let God.'' This is an appropriate time to do that very thing. Let go of insecurities and let God use your life for His glory.
* On a small sheet of paper, write verses on who you are in Christ. On the top of the page write, ''I am a child of the King of the Universe.'' Place the paper where you are certain to see it at least once a day. You could fill a sun visor in your car with such verses to flip down and read at stoplights! Repeat the words, use them in prayer, and make them become a part of your life.

TRY THESE SCRIPTURES TO GET YOU STARTED:

Matthew 5:13,14	Romans 8:1
John 8:31-33	1 Corinthians 6:19
Romans 1:7; Philippians 1:1	2 Corinthians 3:18; Philippians 1:6
Romans 6:2,11	2 Corinthians 5:17,20,21
Galatians 2:20	Galatians 3:9
Colossians 3:12; Romans 1:7	Hebrews 9:14
Ephesians 1:6,7,13	1 Peter 1:16; Ephesians 1:4
Ephesians 2:5,10,19	1 Peter 1:18,19; Galatians 3:13
Ephesians 6:10	1 Peter 1:23
Philippians 2:5	1 Peter 2:24
1 Corinthians 2:16	2 Peter 1:4
Phillipians 4:13	1 John 5:4
Colossians 2:8	Revelation 21:7
Colossians 3:3	

SHE SAID:
''I have found that the more we are identified with Christ, the more freedom we have from the pressures of other people's images of us.''

''How do you find your identity in Christ? You find it by allowing Him to show you your own heart, then by purifying your heart so that you become the same, inside and out.''

— Nancy Corbett Cole[3]

HE SAID:

"When it comes to Christianity, identification is the basic issue. Knowledge of who you are in Christ is edifying. There is nothing more thrilling than to stand in the righteousness of God and declare your identity with Christ. Men have no copyright on that."

— Edwin Louis Cole[4]

LET'S PRAY:

Father, I thank You for creating me in Your image. Help me to be perfected into the image of Jesus; help me to see myself as You see me — not as I see myself, or even as the world sees me. Then if there are things I must change, show me what those things are — and give me the courage and the discipline and the ability to make the changes. Please heal me from a poor self-image and change my perspective into Your perspective of me. I thank You, Father, that You can do through me what I cannot do alone. In Jesus' name I pray. Amen.

MEDITATION:

"For you died, and your life is now hidden with Christ in God."

— Colossians 3:3 NIV

QUOTABLE QUOTES:

"No one can make you feel inferior without your consent."
— *Anna Eleanor Roosevelt[5]*
(1884-1962)

"When one is a stranger to oneself then one is estranged from others too."
— *Anne Morrow Lindbergh[6]*

"The grace of God's presence, the inner calm that comes from encounter with Him, brings me ever closer to attaining my likeness to God lost by original sin."
— *Susan Muto[7]*

THINK ABOUT IT:

"It is our place to remember what we are, in ourselves, in order to appreciate all that we are in Christ!"

— Anne Ortlund[8]

"Jesus shows us that our self-image, our sense of worth, our understanding of who we are must be rooted in God's Word. How we happen to feel about ourselves on a particular morning has nothing to do with it."

— Anne Ortlund[9]

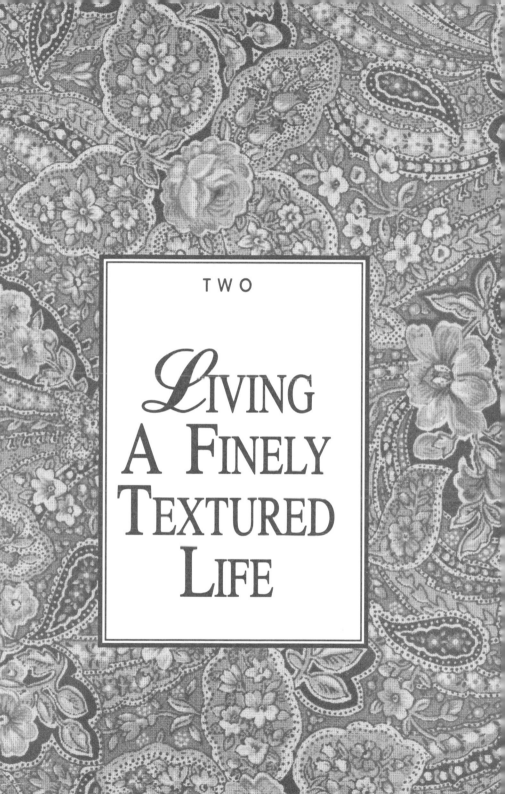

TWO

LIVING A FINELY TEXTURED LIFE

HOSPITALITY:
Forget the Imperfections

What a warm feeling we get from good hospitality! Good hosts and hostesses leave us with a glow that remains for hours. On the other hand, because of our attitudes, extending hospitality ourselves can bring a dark cloud over our head that stays until the last guest leaves. This need not be! We often think a lot is expected of us because of what we have seen others do, but what makes for really good entertaining is to be relaxed as ourselves, whether with paper plates or china and crystal.

One of the nicest gatherings I ever attended was a simple buffet with cold cuts, rolls, store-bought potato salad and a small cake for dessert. What made it remarkable was the simplicity. The hostess showed in every way that we were there for no other reason than to enjoy our friendship, share common concerns, and get to know each other better. Following her lead, we shed all pretense and just enjoyed.

How often have you said, "But my house is a mess, my furniture is old, the carpet is worn out. I couldn't possibly have people in my home!" By adopting this attitude, we rob ourselves of the simple pleasure of giving, of strengthening friendships and meeting new friends. Remember, "If you wait for perfect conditions, you will never get anything done."[1] It's true in hospitality as in all of life.

Some people panic at cooking for others. I'll tell you something I have learned: people who eat home-cooking regularly don't expect more than that, and people who dine out often actually prefer something that tastes home-cooked. When Edwin and I travel for weeks on end, eating constantly in restaurants, I find myself looking forward to a simple meatloaf!

When your guests are people of character, they are not looking at the quality of food, the hole in the carpet, or the worn furniture. They are looking at you, and choosing to know you better. Don't let pride cut you off from new friendships. Relax! And your guests will, too. In the warmth of relationship, you'll forget all imperfections and enjoy yourself!

ACTION STEPS

* Plan your parties well. Make a time-line to ensure you can complete everything with time to spare for relaxing and freshening up before guests arrive. My daughter and I have been known to forget part of the dinner and leave it in the refrigerator. She now makes a list far ahead of time of everything that is to be set out when guests arrive. Double checking the list lets her know her work is over, and she can fully relax with her friends.

* If you always feel like you have to do too much to entertain, try some spontaneity. Call a close friend on the day you want to get together, and come up with a meal using what each of you has on hand. Let her bring over some ingredients, and get everyone involved in making the meal. Some of entertaining's greatest moments are in the kitchen!

* RELAX! Tenseness creates tension in everyone. Just before a party one year, my punchbowl broke, spewing sticky punch all over the table and floor. I learned then how to relax and flow with situations. Guests pitched in to help clean up the mess and it actually served as an ice-breaker! Another time my garbage disposal sort of exploded just before guests arrived so they saw minced food strewn all over. Turn those situations into reasons for laughter. Watch as people heave a sigh of relief and laugh with you!

* Hospitality is a required prerequisite for leadership. God would not ask you to do it if you couldn't! The Bible says: ''He [a leader] must enjoy having guests in his home.''[2]

QUOTABLE QUOTES:

''Nature, like Us is sometimes caught
Without her Diadem.''

> — *Emily Dickinson*[3]
> *(1830-1886)*

''How many cares one loses when one decides not to be something but to be someone.''
> — *Remark by Coco Chanel*[4]

SMILE:
All the Medicine You Need

There is nothing so contagious as a smile or a laugh. Just thinking of friends who have a gift for laughter brings a smile to my lips. Hearing laughter before you walk into a room can quicken your pace and lift your spirits. "A merry heart doeth good like a medicine."[1] The noted psychologist, Dr. Norman Cousins, proved this when he faced a terminal illness. He discovered that his condition improved when he laughed, so he started setting aside time for laughter.[2] Before long he was well!

Laughter was almost all the medicine he needed.

I remember getting into an elevator in a strange city. A lady got in after me, smiled directly at me and said, "Good morning." As I smiled back, I no longer felt strange or alone. Today I still remember her smile. It was warm, bright, and seemed to signal a pleasant day ahead. It is funny how something as simple as a smile makes people feel "like a million" though it doesn't cost a cent.

Adding more smiles to our homes solidifies our love. Why let the family know how worried, frustrated or irritated you are about circumstances? When things are bad, think on the good things of life. The negative will eventually go away. We can certainly choose in the meantime to have a smile on our lips and joy in our heart.

We know the Savior, and He is more than ready to handle any problem no matter how big it seems to us. Smiling just seems to lighten the load.

ACTION STEPS
* Meditate on this verse: Psalm 97:11 "Light is sown for the righteous, and gladness for the upright in heart." Thank God for the light that dispels darkness. Receive His "gladness" for the "upright" that does not depend on outside circumstances.

- There is an old song that goes, "Accentuate the positive, eliminate the negative, latch on to the affirmative, don't mess with Mr. In-between."[3] (This sounds a lot like Philippians 4:11.) It was recently revived in some popular films and advertisements. I taught it to my daughter when she was going through particularly trying, life-or-death circumstances, and it helped her keep her perspective. Write it out and keep it somewhere visible until it really sinks in.
- Choose a week in which you will concentrate on smiling at home. Smile heartily at your children and spouse as soon as you see them, every time you look at them. See if there is not a distinct mood change around your home! Then try to make it a habit!

WORTH QUOTING:

"Celebrating each new day helps us develop the ability to be grateful for all new moments and for the God Who is in each one."

— Karen Burton Mains[4]

GRACIOUSNESS:
The Art of Living

A s I stepped off the train, the glow of neon lights, smells of foods proffered by street vendors, rush of traffic and blaring of horns startled me. Japan! What a disturbing, exciting, dignified, curious country. I was visiting my daughter, Joann, who taught English as a missions effort in a rural community, and we had taken three trains en route to visit her friend, Jill, in the urban sprawl of Osaka.

Joann quickly dragged our luggage to a box-like telephone and dialed a number. Within minutes a sedan pulled up and out bounced Jill, a petite, young American mother of three. We crowded in and Jill chatted with a constant smile as she navigated the narrow, unlit streets to her home, passing oncoming cars so closely that I leaned the opposite direction trying unconsciously to avoid an accident.

I learned that Jill taught English and Bible classes in homes and, since her husband worked typically long Japanese hours, she raised their children almost alone. She immersed them in American culture, while respecting her host country and encouraging them to speak Japanese. She managed a tiny budget for that economy, hoarding American cooking ingredients so she could entertain with treats from home. The day we arrived, she took a Japanese dinner to a sick student, worked, and still managed to make an American dinner for us, complete with chocolate cake.

Sunday morning, I awoke to see her bringing in laundry off the clothesline. I was amazed to see that she was finishing her laundry on a Sunday morning with three children to dress for church, but I was shocked when I realized she laundered everything, cloth diapers and all, with only a wringer washer and clothesline. When she saw me staring at her, she buried her nose in the armload of clothes, took a deep breath, and said, "Don't you just love the smell of line-dried clothes?"

Jill had the grace of spirit that clothes Christ's truest disciples. His grace transcends the mundane, the boring, the tedious times in our lives and brings out the riches God has placed in us.

The word, *gracious,* is defined as graceful, merciful, compassionate, marked by kindness, courtesy, tact, delicacy, charm, good taste and generosity of spirit. Seeing Jill make the most of every day on foreign soil, and making light of every obstacle, I felt I had met a "gracious" woman. I know of no one who actually embodies all these virtues all the time, but Jill's life proves we can come close!

ACTION STEPS

* Becoming aware of something is often the only motivation needed to become that something. To become a gracious woman, try listing the ways in which you already extend graciousness. Then, list the ways in which you could be more gracious, and stay aware of them.
* Be observant of others: you can pick up dozens of ideas from the gracious actions of those around you. You don't need to mimic, just notice things that stand out, and begin to incorporate them into your life in your own way. For example, offer tea instead of coffee some of the time and serve it in your nicest china. Write thank-you notes profusely. Take a card and perhaps a small gift to a neighbor who had a baby, or to an acquaintance in the hospital. Cook a dinner dish for a friend's family when she is sick. These are all generous acts of kindness that will mark you as a gracious woman!
* In what ways was Jesus Christ gracious? Look at this list of definitions again:
— graceful, merciful, compassionate. Marked by: kindness, courtesy, tact, delicacy, charm, good taste and generosity of spirit. Doesn't each one of these qualities describe our Lord? Remember how He cooked fish for the disciples? How He washed their feet? And He always had time to play with children, comfort the bereaved, listen to concerns. Becoming more like Jesus will naturally make us more gracious!

SHE SAID:

"If we go out of our way to help others and minister to them, and do it as unto the Lord, we deserve His reward, not just our earthly rewards of gratitude from others."
— Nancy Corbett Cole[1]

HE SAID:

"Exterior beauty cannot compare with internal loveliness."
— Edwin Louis Cole[2]

LET'S PRAY:

Father, I desire to develop the art of gracious living. In Jesus' name, I ask You now to fill me with the grace of Your dear Son, that I might in turn be gracious with others. As You teach me, Lord, help me to be willing to use what You teach me in my daily living, in a way that blesses my family and others. In Jesus' name, I thank You for hearing and answering my heart's prayer today. Amen.

QUOTABLE:

"The whole person is involved in being a Christian. The whole life is involved in living in contact with God."

— Edith Schaeffer[3]

SINGLE:
"One" by One

Much of the Bible's writing and duplicating, hundreds of missionary efforts, and many great institutions resulted from a single person being single-minded to accomplish one thing. Many women are single by choice — perhaps they enjoy it, or are devoted only to God or a noble cause. But many single women yearn to be fulfilled in relationship to a man through marriage.

"Even the animals on the ark went two by two!" a single woman may lament. "Why isn't there someone for me?" This can be God's desire placed in a single woman's heart for Him to fulfill (Ps. 37:4), but it can also be a warning sign.

The danger for single women is to feel lost, like they don't have an identity unless they are with a man. The truth is, building an identity around a person is wrong for singles, just as it is for married women. Our identity is not based on a husband, child, career, house or car. Our identity is based on Jesus Christ — in Whose image we were created, through Whose sacrifice we received new life, and by Whose power He fulfills the potential He placed within us when He created us in our mothers' wombs! This is some identity!

We are created complete as a "one" by One Who does all things perfectly. No wonder so many singles can live happily fulfilled lives. The more we become like our Creator, the closer we are to His original design for us, so the more "ourselves" we really are.

If you are single, look to your loving Savior to "find" yourself. Become fulfilled by allowing God to maximize the potential He placed within you. And think of your blessings, not your hardships. The Bible says that a single woman invests her time in serving the Lord, but the married woman can be distracted by her husband (and children, cooking, cleaning, etc.) (1 Cor. 7:34.) If you are single, you can do so much that a married woman simply cannot do.

Find what God has for you and become a valuable, fulfilled, contributing person right where you are.

ACTION STEPS

- God is concerned about single women. If you are single, look up Isaiah 54:1-8; Jeremiah 49:11; and Hosea 14:3, and let your heart rejoice that God is looking out for you!
- Thoughts for singles to resist:
  - Don't think something is wrong with you! Submit yourself to the Lord and He will "direct your paths"[1] and change you "from glory to glory."[2] He will prepare you to be the perfect person for your future spouse, just as carefully as He is preparing your future spouse to be the perfect person for you.
  - Don't think you have to hurry. God's timing is always the right timing, regardless of what those around you might say.
  - Don't think you have to go to the marketplace to find "him." Go wherever and do whatever God instructs, and He will make your paths cross. The niece I talked about in "Waiting" was sick at home when God brought her husband to her door. A friend of mine was teaching a children's Sunday School class when God's man for her walked in and said God told him to help with the children!
  - Don't be confused about whether someone is "Mr. Right." God will clearly lead you. Ask Him for confirmation through His Word and godly counsel. Confusion is not from the Lord.
  - Don't think God is unfair to keep you waiting. If you are single year after year, thank God for spending that extra time to make you all you can be![3]
  - Don't think you have to become an excellent "date." How much better to be friends with an assortment of men, and part of a fun-loving group most of the time! Keep your emotions free so your spirit can hear from God.
- Thoughts for singles to accept:
  - Stay completely focused on God. Many women think in terms of the "ideal" man. After marriage, when the "real" meets the "ideal," the amount of difference between the two is the amount of trouble she has in adjusting.
  - Think of what God has done in your life recently. Have you purchased a car in your favorite color, foods you desired, clothes that pleased you? Have you scheduled your day, stayed up late reading, rearranged your furniture? Have you planned a vacation, even traveled on a missionary trip you wouldn't have been free to take had you been married? Live it up! Promise yourself to enjoy these benefits while they last, and to enjoy just as much the other set of benefits that marriage brings. All we really do when we marry is exchange one set of benefits and handicaps for another.
  - Think about where you need work! You are in an excellent position to build character. During any marriage, the amount of money you have (or don't have), the color the bridesmaids' dresses were at the wedding, and where you decide to live are far less critical than the things you have built into your own character which follow you everywhere. Good character comes through daily communion with the Lord in prayer and reading the Word.

SHE SAID:

"Single women usually have the best opportunity of all to get an education and learn a profession. They can be ready to step in if need be and provide an adequate living for their family. This is not a new 'pro-woman' attitude. It is as old as history. The Proverbs 31 woman was equal to any task."

— Nancy Corbett Cole[4]

HE SAID:

"The greatest danger for a single woman in contemplating marriage is 'mythical mating,' or 'magical thinking.' To marry with the idea that she will live some kind of charmed, carefree life is to entertain a myth."

— Edwin Louis Cole[5]

LET'S PRAY:

Father, Help me to be all that I can be, to change what I can change, and to accept the identity You give me. I know there is no one like me so please help me to accept myself, single, in the state in which You created me. Take all frustration from me, and all fear. Give me the grace to wait, in purity, for that special one You may prepare for me to marry. In Jesus' name I pray. Amen.

QUOTABLE:

" *'Tain't worthwhile to wear a day all out before it comes."*

— *Sarah Orne Jewett[6]*
(1849-1909)

TALENTS:
Too Much To Cram Into Thirty Years

I have known my daughter-in-law, Judi, since she was a teenager. Watching her grow into a mature and creative adult has been a pleasure. She is a successful singer, wife, mother, and dress designer. Her home where she often hosts Bible studies is a masterpiece design of her creation.

We are all generally proud of our children, but I say this about Judi because I remember when she felt like she could do very little, and had few talents to offer the Lord. The truth is, God has given talents to each of us. We cannot all sing or design a home that looks like Judi's, but we can develop the talents God gives us for His glory.

At a church Edwin and I pastored, a mature woman trained the younger ladies in the fine art of entertaining, from the making of tea sandwiches to the setting of an elegant table. She didn't consciously start out saying, "I'm going to teach people how to do things right." But having learned what she was personally interested in, her talent evolved into a special function that trained perhaps a hundred women to entertain large crowds. In churches, this is an especially admired talent!

I have seen shy, insecure women who could not hold a conversation with someone, faithfully apply themselves to God's Word and prayer. Gradually, I have seen them grow in confidence and win their friends and neighbors to Jesus Christ. What could be a more rewarding talent to develop?

Life is an ongoing process, a gradual growth in grace and in the talents God has placed within us. The talents we use change from season to season so there is a lifetime to develop them. God will bring to the surface at the proper time talents that laid dormant for years.

You need never say, "What's the use now — my life is half over?" As we press into

God, we realize that what He has for us is far too much to cram into the first thirty, forty, or fifty years of our lives.

"There is a time for everything,"[1] the Bible says, so keep looking for and developing new talents. God will bring them out in you, as you yield yourself to Him.

ACTION STEPS

* Develop those talents that have been lying dormant! Enroll in that college course you always wanted to take. Learn a new language, or learn how to say at least "Good Morning" in ten languages.
* Do you have unfulfilled desire in your heart? Take it to the Lord in prayer and find out what His schedule is right now. As the seasons of life pass, accept what desires He is fulfilling right here and now. Perhaps He wants you to concentrate on work, or your husband, or your children right now. You have to find that out by yourself in prayer.

MEDITATIONS:

"Delight thyself also in the Lord; and he shall give thee the desires of thine heart. Commit they way unto the Lord; trust also in him; and he shall bring it to pass."
— Psalm 37:4,5

"Genius is an infinite capacity for taking pains."
— Jane Ellice Hopkins[2]
(1836-1904)

ADDICTIONS:
Overcome by Prayer

So many women today have habits they are unable to break. If you are one, there is hope!

My friend, Sandy, was a compulsive person with many destructive addictions: alcohol, food, shopping, etc. She ended up in a mental institution and later wrote about her experiences in a wonderful book, *The Compulsive Woman*.[1]

When Sandy was hospitalized, unbeknownst to her, a small band of women prayed for her regularly. One night in the hospital a young weeping woman wandered into Sandy's room to ask if Jesus loved her. Sandy comforted the girl by saying, "Yes, Jesus loves you." Instantly, memories of Sandy's church upbringing stirred Sandy to call on the Lord. God heard and answered and soon Sandy was released to resume her life. It was not easy, but with all her heart she sought deliverance and God provided it.

Occasionally God delivers a person from addictions overnight. Sandy struggled valiantly for months with the help of many supporters before overcoming them. Regardless of the means of deliverance, we all must determine in our hearts, "I WILL live for God, I will NOT be dragged into that pit again." A different environment, godly friends and counsel, the power of prayer, and a determination to do right will lead us out of a despairing existence.

Sandy now tours the country lecturing on compulsions. At the end of her lecture she tells a big secret: After writing her book, Sandy sent copies to everyone who was important in her life. When she contacted the mental hospital to find the address of the woman who awakened her in the night, they had no record of any such person. Sandy believes God answered the prayers of the small band of women by sending an angel to her hospital room!

ACTION STEPS

- Do you have habits in your life you consider addictive? Ask God in prayer to help you overcome them. He helped Sandy do it, and He will do the same for you!
- Do you have a friend who is addicted? Overweight? Compulsive? Instead of criticizing her, band together with one or two other women and commit yourselves to prayer. Pray daily or choose a specific day of the week. If you cannot be together, just agree in prayer in your own private prayer time.
- Regardless of how far down you sink, remember Jesus ministered to the lowliest people on earth — He is right there where you are! Write out Scriptures that apply to you and hang them on your wall or mirror. Recite them daily and trust God to make them a reality in your life, such as:
- 2 Corinthians 5:17: "If any man be in Christ, he is a new creature: old things are passed away; behold, all things are become new." 2 Corinthians 5:21: "For he hath made him to be sin for us, who knew no sin; that we might be made the righteousness of God in him."
- Seek out groups in your community that offer programs for your habit, addiction or problem. They can help!

SHE SAID:

"There is no reason why you cannot become all God created you to be. You can be as great as any biblical hero or heroine, but there are obstacles you will have to overcome just as they did . . . . But, if you can become convinced in your heart that God loves you, nothing can stop you from achieving His purposes for your life."

— Nancy Corbett Cole[2]

HE SAID:

"Thank God we never lose His love. He said so. He said that we have left it, not lost it, therefore it can be regained."

— Edwin Louis Cole[3]

FOOD FOR THOUGHT:

"These things I have spoken unto you, that in me ye might have peace. In the world ye shall have tribulation: but be of good cheer; I have overcome the world."

— John 16:33

"For I am convinced that neither death nor life, neither angels nor demons, neither the present nor the future, nor any powers, neither height nor depth, nor anything else in all creation, will be able to separate us from the love of God that is in Christ Jesus our Lord."

— Romans 8:38,39 NIV

QUOTABLE

"Courage is the price that life exacts for granting peace.
The soul that knows it not, knows no release
From little things;
Knows not the livid loneliness of fear,
Nor mountain heights where bitter joy can hear
The sounds of wings."

— *Amelia Earhart Putnam*[4]

"We never know how high we are
Till we are called to rise
And then, if we are true to plan
Our statures touch the skies."

— *Emily Dickinson*[5]

TIME:
Controlling the Clock

E veryone has wasted a minute, an hour, or a day and lived to regret it. God gives us twenty-four hours every day, but some are better at managing them than others. I have concluded that if we want to accomplish anything, we will never *find* time, we have to *make* time.

A friend of mine was called on to speak once for a women's gathering. She had written out her notes, intending to type them, when something came up and she decided she did not have time for typing. To her chagrin, when she stood in the lectern, she found the lighting in the auditorium insufficient to illumine her scribbles. God graciously helped her as she fumbled through, but she was humbled into a new determination to control time. Since then, she has become a well-known (and well organized) public speaker.

I have learned three simple lessons about controlling time:

— *"To do" lists give peace of mind.* I use the pen and paper on my bedside table at night as I fall asleep, and in the morning when I awaken. Particularly at prayer time, things pop into my mind that need to be done. If I have a pen and paper, it is so easy to jot things down as they come to mind, and I can then concentrate on prayer more easily. This increases the peace of a night's rest, and greatly enhances prayer.

— *When you start to do things on your list, do easy things first.* If you have six easy chores and two harder or more complicated tasks, do the easy ones first. This gives a sense of accomplishment and enables you to concentrate on the harder or more time-consuming tasks.

— *Beware, television is a thief!* Watch that thief or it will steal your time and the peace from your home.

Our twenty-four hours are precious and can never be regained. We must learn to control them wisely.

ACTION STEPS
* Put a pen and paper next to your bed. Make a habit of jotting down notes, then slip them into your purse every day. Voila! You will never forget again!
* Turn off the television! If you are really hooked:
  — Write programs on the left side of a piece of paper, then what you gain from them on the right. If all you are gaining is something to talk about with others, turn them off!
  — For one week, use the time you normally watch TV to read, study, pray, serve others, take up a sport, write letters, learn a hobby, or just do everything a little better. (Do not switch from a TV habit to a telephone habit!) Keep track on paper of all the things you accomplish that week with the TV off. Those are the things you were robbed of before!

LET'S PRAY:
Lord, help me to organize my time according to Your priorities for me and my family. Give me the ability to use time wisely, I pray, in Jesus' name. Amen.

WORTH QUOTING:
"The most precious thing a human being has to give is time. There is so very little of it, after all, in a life."
> — *Edith Schaeffer*[1]

"I'll tell you how the sun rose —
A ribbon at a time —"
> — *Emily Dickinson*[2]
> *(1830-1886)*

"No time like the present."
> — *Mary de la Riviere Manley*[3]
> *(1663-1724)*

FAMILY TRADITIONS:
Making Meaningful Memories

D o you have family traditions such as family reunions, special foods or birthday parties? Most family traditions promote togetherness and solidify interpersonal relations.

A very simple tradition for our family was to have baked apples on Christmas morning. Two years ago at Christmas, our entire family traveled to the small town where my daughter, Lois, had moved. We took over all five bedrooms of a bed and breakfast establishment, and had the run of the house. On Christmas morning thirteen of us crowded around the dining table and our jaws dropped when the host served baked apples! I felt twice blessed, not only having my whole family there but having the traditional breakfast that our children grew up with.

We also had traditions of family prayer time and "Family Council," which my children remember fondly. Now that the children are all adults, we are still holding, changing, and adding traditions. There are some family traditions, however, which are unproductive. My friend, Sheila, used to cut off the end of a ham before putting it in a pot to cook. Her mother taught her this. One day she was at her grandmother's when her grandmother fixed a ham.

"Grandma," she asked, "Why do you always cut off the end of the ham to cook it?"

"Because my pot's too small for the whole ham," came the abrupt response.

Sheila burst out laughing. Two generations had followed suit before they realized it wasn't necessary to cut the ham if they had a bigger pot than Grandma did!

This made Sheila start questioning other things she did, in cooking, raising children, cleaning house — everything. She realized how guilty she felt for not always doing or enjoying everything her mother did. She began wondering if her mother had really enjoyed doing all she did. Sheila now takes the time to scrutinize her routines objectively, which has alleviated a great deal of guilt.

Family traditions are important to family unity and our children's security, but if we have traditions that don't serve that purpose, it is time to break them! If you have a large pot, cook the whole ham!

ACTION STEPS

• Develop meaningful and godly traditions. Go through a calendar and see what kinds of traditions you have established. Choose new traditions you would like to add. Check with your husband, if you are married, and see if any of his family's traditions could be resurrected.

• Teach small children your traditions, and their roles in them. This provides security now, and serves a larger purpose later, when as teenagers they strive for independence. It's easy to draw teens back into your family circle and give them the security they need by doing the traditional thing they are accustomed to.

• Spend a few days, or even a week, questioning your routines. Ask yourself if there is an easier way, or if you are plagued by guilt from not doing things as Mother did them. Decide how you will do things in the future, and be free from guilt and the past! Traditions are not an end in themselves. They are not to be followed legalistically, superstitiously, or unquestioningly.

• Think practically! What national holidays could your family start a tradition about? Find something meaningful to encourage participation, then teach your children what a big, wonderful heritage is theirs!

THE FAMILY THAT PRAYS TOGETHER . . .[1]

In his book, *My Answer,* evangelist Billy Graham lists seven reasons why he believes family devotions are important. They are:

1. It unifies the home life, and puts faith in the place of friction.

2. It brings to the family group a sense of God's presence.

3. It shows the children that God is relevant to everyday living, and not just a Being to be worshiped on Sunday.

4. It gives members of the family an opportunity for self-examination and confession of sin.

5. It strengthens the members of the household for the tasks and the responsibilities they are to face during the day.

6. It insulates us against the hurts and misunderstandings which come our way.

7. It supplements the work of the church, and makes our homes a sanctuary where Christ is honored.

QUOTABLE QUOTES:

"America! America!
God shed His grace on thee."
>— *Katherine Lee Bates*[2]
>*(1859-1929)*

"Ay, call it holy ground,
The soil where first they trod!
They have left unstained what there they found —
Freedom to worship God."
>— *Felicia Dorothea Hemans*[3]
>*(1793-1835)*

THREE

HEART STRINGS

FORGIVENESS:
The Fresh Start

While sorting through a stack of mail, familiar handwriting begged me to open a letter immediately. It was "long-lost" Beth, saying she would visit next month. I was excited, but I wondered . . . .

Beth and I met at a tennis match years earlier. We were friends when she and her husband began their Christian walk, and stayed close until they moved far away to a rural community. There, without the Bible studies, Christian friends, and churches they were such a part of, their love for the Lord grew cold. As they loved the Lord less, they loved each other less, and eventually divorced. It was rather easy because they had no children.

Later, Beth's mother died and Beth returned home to find that her brother had usurped the estate and would have nothing to do with her. Part of a small family to begin with, she now had no relations at all. For years I didn't hear again from her . . . until now.

When Beth arrived, she told me of her futile attempts to reconcile with her husband and brother. She had faltered through life, but when she broke off a relationship with a man, she suddenly awoke to the realization that she had no one to lean on, no one to love, and was betrayed by all. She hovered between taking her life and trying to salvage it. Thanks to a faithful God, she chose to salvage it.

During her visit, Beth gave her heartache to the Lord, and found she was not alone in the family of God; something draws us closer than human relatives — the blood of Jesus; something overpowers human emotions — the love of God; something releases every restraint — the forgiveness of God. When Beth acknowledged that Jesus didn't condemn her, but was waiting with open arms, she was transformed.

The Bible says, "If you forgive the sins of any, they are forgiven them; if you retain the sins of any, they are retained."[1]

Beth knew from her Christian training that to become completely free from the build-up of sin, she needed to release the sins of others, in the same way Christ forgave her. She began by forgiving her ex-husband and brother, then tackled the hardest of all — forgiving herself.

Today Beth is back where God wants her. She has turned from the past and is looking confidently to the future, surrounded by loving, Christian friends. She has learned that forgiveness releases, and more importantly, that God forgives!

ACTION STEPS

* Break through the barriers between you and God erected by unforgiveness! Forgiveness for EVERY sin is yours just for the asking! Jesus looked down from the cross and said, "Father, forgive them."[2] In that simple prayer, He forgave every one of us throughout the history of mankind. Accept that forgiveness for every mistake you ever made. "If we confess our sins, he is faithful and just to forgive us our sins, and to cleanse us from all unrighteousness."[3]
* Forgiving others is an obedient step of faith, not a feeling. Learn to understand forgiveness in the light of God's Word:
  1. Forgiveness is a step of *obedience* because God commands us to forgive.
  2. Forgiveness is a step of *faith,* because we often do not feel forgiving, nor do we recognize the importance of forgiving.
  3. When Jesus said, "Whosoever sins ye do not forgive, they are retained," He meant that sins you personally do not forgive continue to live on. This is why we often begin to act like the person we didn't forgive.
  4. The reason we forgive even though we don't "feel" anything is because emotions follow actions. When we obediently ACT by forgiving, we can trust God that the emotions will one day come.
* Any time you feel far from God, go back and do your "first works" over again. "But I have this against you, that you have left your first love. Remember therefore from where you have fallen, and repent and do the deeds you did at first."[4] This means, start at the point of salvation. Study what salvation means, really repent of sins — both known and unknown, pour your heart out to God as if you just discovered His existence. See if this doesn't stir new life within your heart!
* If you have never received Christ's forgiveness, turn to "A Final Word" at the back of this book so that you can get started today on your new life.

LET'S PRAY:

Father, You know what is in my heart. You know the mistakes, sins, errors I have made. I ask You to forgive me for them. God, You also know the wounds, hurts, and all that I need to forgive others for. So right now by faith, I forgive that person, those people, who sinned against me. I trust You, Lord, to take care of them, and of me, so that one day I would no longer have any emotions other than total freedom from those situations.

I do this as an act of obedience today, because I want to love and follow You. In Jesus' name I pray. Amen.

JUST A THOUGHT:
"For a long moment, we grasped each other's hands, the former guard and the former prisoner. I had never known God's love so intensely as I did then. But even so, I realized it was not my love. I had tried, and did not have the power. It was the power of the Holy Spirit as recorded in Romans 5:5, ' . . . because the love of God is shed abroad in our hearts by the Holy Ghost which is given to us.' "
— Corrie ten Boom[5]
former Nazi concentration camp
prisoner

HE SAID:
"Emotions follow actions. To change your emotions, change your actions."
— Edwin Louis Cole[6]

SHE SAID:
"Forgiveness is the key to breaking the cycle of sins passed from one generation to another. Forgiveness is the key to submitting to the love of your heavenly Father and the love of those around you."
— Nancy Corbett Cole[7]

WORTH QUOTING:
"Better by far you should forget and smile
Than you should remember and be sad."
— *Christina Georgina Rossetti*[8]
(1830-1894)

FAITH AND FINANCES:
$7.00 and a Fruitcake

When Edwin and I first launched into ministry, it was truly a walk of faith. I was a young pregnant mother when Edwin heard God's call to full-time ministry. Immediately he left his job, so to cut expenses we moved to another city into an apartment.

We were committed to the Lord, but we needed faith for those elusive finances that have stymied many a budding ministry. Our only income was meager offerings from rarely offered preaching engagements.

Shortly before Christmas, with our second child due in three months, Edwin held services at a country church. When he came home a few days before Christmas, I hoped for something to pay my doctor and buy gifts. I expected at least enough for groceries. Instead, he came home with $7.00 and a fruitcake! It seems funny today, but at the time my faith hit rock bottom.

"Seven dollars and a fruitcake, Lord?!" As I poured out my woes to the Lord the next day, I heard Him distinctly say, "Lo, I am with you always."[1] I looked up to see my mother-in-law walking up the long driveway outside my window and for an instant I wondered if she heard it, too. Then I realized God had spoken to me, just me, and such peace overwhelmed me! When God is with us, what can harm us?

By Christmas, Edwin had found a good secular job, we paid the physician and Lois was born in March. After much prayer and soul-searching, we asked God to put us in full-time ministry by June 1. Then, through some seemingly ordinary circumstances, we began pastoring a lovely country church on June 1! Our faith soared! God proved to me two things: He is always with us just as His Word says. And, God always finishes what He authors, but according to His timetable, not ours.

God will see you through financial distress as well as every other problem. There is nothing too big for our God to handle. Put your faith in Him and He will provide!

ACTION STEPS

- Even when the worst financial distress comes, God is still with you. So, pray! He will provide a way for you. First Corinthians 10:3 (NIV) says: "They all ate the same spiritual food . . . ."

- God does not do what we expect, He does what is right. Just because your expectations are not met, do not give up on God. He is always working for your highest good. Die to those expectations, and become alive only to what the Holy Spirit is really doing. Second Corinthians 10:5 (NIV) says: "We demolish arguments and every pretension that sets itself up against the knowledge of God, and we take captive every thought to make it obedient to Christ."

- Turn your worst nightmares into your best memories by pressing into God in prayer. Set time aside for yourself to get alone with Him. After you have poured out your heart, start focusing on His goodness. Read Scriptures out loud about His goodness to you, and convince your mind what your spirit already knows — that God is a GOOD Heavenly Father. Think about these scriptures:
  - Psalm 25:8 (NIV): "Good and upright is the Lord; therefore he instructs sinners in his ways."
  - Psalm 27:14 (NIV): "Wait for the Lord; be strong and take heart and wait for the Lord."
  - Psalm 31:24 (NIV): "Be strong and take heart, all you who hope in the Lord."
  - Psalm 34:8 (NIV): "Taste and see that the Lord is good; blessed is the man who takes refuge in him."

- View disappointments as learning experiences and they will become stepping stones to a successful life.
  - Proverbs 15:13 (NIV): "A happy heart makes the face cheerful, but heartache crushes the spirit."

HE SAID:

As a practical reminder of the principles of handling money, refer often to the list below:[2]

1. God is your source.
2. Seek God first in everything.
3. Decisions require responsibility. Decisions cannot be unilateral in marriage.
4. Tithing is basic visible evidence of faith.
5. Get out of debt.
6. Start where you are with what you have.
7. Live within your means.
8. To obey God today is to trust Him for tomorrow.
9. Keep adequate records.
10. Be generous with God — and with others.

LET'S PRAY:

Father, I thank You that You are faithful to hear and answer prayer. You know the struggles I am having right now with my finances. Help me to understand more fully Your Word regarding financial principles. Give me wisdom, Lord, to put those principles into daily practice. Help me to see my finances through the eyes of faith, and if I am making things complicated, I ask You to help me to keep things simple. Make my paths straight, Lord. I ask for Your guidance in all my family's financial affairs. In Jesus' name I pray. Amen.

MEDITATION:

"Seek ye first the kingdom of God, and his righteousness; and all these things shall be added unto you."

— Matthew 6:33

WORTH QUOTING:

" 'Twant me, 'twas the Lord. I always told Him, 'I trust You. I don't know where to go or what to do, but I expect You to lead me,' and He always did."

— *Harriett Tubman*[3]
(1823-1913)

"God answers sharp and sudden on some prayers, And thrusts the thing we have prayed for in our face, A gauntlet with a gift in 't."

— *Elizabeth Barrett Browning*[4]
(1806-1861)

WAITING:
God's Unexpected Answers

Have you ever lacked direction? Sometimes, you just need to keep on with whatever you are doing until God intervenes.

Carol is a favorite niece of mine. Naturally bright and energetic, all she seemed to lack was direction when, in her late teens, she came for a two-week visit to our home one summer. Edwin teases her still, but it did not surprise me that the two weeks stretched to three years with Carol completing college before returning home.

In college, Carol drew close to the Lord, but not to any of the eligible men around her. She was physically fit, beautiful, a gourmet cook and an exceptional student who seemed destined to enter a successful career. But I sensed that inside she was unfulfilled and still lacked direction, and I sometimes wondered about her indifference to dating.

How silly to underestimate God's plans for His saints!

Carol returned home from her "visit" and did temporary work until an automobile accident left her bedridden for several weeks. When a church elder requested prayer for her at church, a young man named Doug decided to visit, though they had only briefly met months earlier. Doug is one of those outgoing people who makes everyone's problem his problem. He regularly mows widows' lawns, runs errands for shut-ins and simply uses his gift of helps wherever he is needed. He was not warmly welcomed when he visited unannounced the first time. But seeing there was a need, he persistently returned and soon a beautiful friendship began which blossomed into romance and marriage. After marrying, Carol earned a master's degree in education, completing her unannounced plan to home school as many children as God would give her! Carol's friends from college can hardly believe she gave up all career plans and settled into the role of a homemaker who now has three adorable children.

What a blessing when we wait on God who knows our heart's desires, and wants what is best for us and for those we love!

ACTION STEPS

* Earnestly seek God through prayer for direction in your life, but do not stop living! King Solomon said to sow your seed both day and night, because you do not know where the profit may come from.[1]
* Practice waiting and keeping a quiet spirit. When you go to prayer today, give all your cares to the Lord, then sit in quiet stillness for about five minutes. Before you resume your activities, praise Him for the answers that are surely on their way!
* Let God surprise you. Do not look at everyone as a potential mate, or an answer to your financial need, or any other need. Just go on living and let God take over.
* Do you have a gift of helps like Doug? Go out and use it! You don't know what kind of blessing you may find.

LET'S PRAY:

Father, please direct my steps according to Your Word. I desire to wait on You, because only You know what's best for me. Please give me patience, and guide me toward the future You have planned for me and away from paths that will take me in other directions. In Jesus' name I pray, thanking You for hearing me. Amen.

QUOTABLE:

"Faith is knowing that troubles do exist, but it is also the trust to know that they're not going to last forever and that you will feel better."
— *Barbara Johnson*[2]

PRAISE:
The Reflection of Love

A book title, *I'm Not Mad at God,* intrigued me once, but I passed it by because I couldn't understand it. Years later God reminded me of a time in my early walk with Him when I simply could not praise Him. Then I remembered that book cover and finally realized how someone could be mad at God, for that is exactly what I had been.

When I became a Christian, all I knew was that Jesus loved me. The thrill of new life lingered for months and I savored the fresh, rich experience with my newly discovered Savior.

But then Edwin entered the ministry, and the next thing I knew I was thrust into the role of a pastor's wife. I knew next to nothing about church life, and was only beginning to understand my own salvation. On top of that, I was a new mother with a baby and toddler, and felt like I would never make it through certain days (other mothers may know what I mean). My darling husband, Edwin, was awed with his first pastorate. He waited on God, prepared sermons, visited the congregation and brought many people to Christ. There is no higher calling than to shepherd a flock, and he was at once humbled and enthralled with the privilege.

But being caught up in it, he did not have much time for me or our children. He tried to be a good husband and father, but many times I felt I needed him more than the church did.

My solution — I grumbled! And the more I grumbled, the more my spirit dried up. Once I had longed to shower my Lord with love and praise, but now there was hardly anything left for Him. I didn't look to Him for help, but wallowed in self-pity. The more I looked at circumstances, the further out the window flew my desire to praise Him. As

79

I continued to try to love Him, feeble and imperfect though it was, God graciously brought me out of that miserable state, and away from a pitfall I was not even aware of.

Now here I was years later, realizing at last that I had been mad at Him. I repented for resenting Him, for being bitter about my husband's ministry, and for ignoring Him in my crisis. Today I watch my praise to God like a barometer, for the exercise of praise reveals to me hidden feelings or sins that I am holding back.

When I praise Him most freely is when my heart is pure of all known sin and I can bask in His love. If we are willing and open to learn what only the Holy Spirit can teach us, our hearts will eventually overflow with praise. The Scripture says that praise is becoming to us.[1]

Have you ever seen someone "glowing" with the love of the Lord? We also are radiant in His eyes when He sees pure hearts, heads thrown back freely, faces beaming, reflecting His love back to Him, and lips filled with nothing but praise for Him. What a better way to go than grumbling!

ACTION STEPS

- Have you never felt the fullness of praise well up within you? Start by purifying your heart of known sin as the Holy Spirit reveals it to you, confessing it as He does. Then read Psalm 145 out loud, repeating the verses that touch your heart the most and make you want to praise God more. Follow with Psalms 144, 147, 148, 149 and 150. Maybe you can take one each day, purifying your heart first, until praise begins to flow out of you like it flowed out of the Psalmist.
- Grumbling will never accomplish what praise will! Is there something that you always grumble about? Praise God today for the fact that He is God, He is bigger than that "thing," and that His Spirit within you is stronger than any "thing" that can come up.
- The next time you have an opportunity to grumble or become angry, try praising God instead. As you praise Him, let yourself see Him in His glory, as the master of all, the Lord of the universe, then with that divine perspective, praise Him in advance for taking that opportunity for "bad" and turning it into something "good."
- Make praise a regular part of your prayer time. If you drive much, or spend a lot of time alone somewhere, make it a habit in the car, or wherever you are. When you are unable to praise, use that as a barometer to discover what is hidden in your heart. When you know the cause, acknowledge that God is bigger than the cause, and let your praises ring!

LET'S PRAY:

Lord, give me a heart of praise. Your Word says You inhabit the praises of Your people; please help me to always find something to praise You for. Thank You for the many blessings You have given to me and my family. Help me to develop the discipline of praising You daily. In Jesus' name. Amen.

WORTH QUOTING:
"There are two ways of spreading light: to be
The candle or the mirror that reflects it."
— Edith Wharton[2]
(1862-1937)

"Beloved, when you have put on your beautiful garments of praise (for no matter how homely you may be to the natural eye, you are beautiful to the Lord when you have put on praise as a garment), you are lifted above your own 'make-up' and 'disposition' and swing far out into the realm of the Spirit."
— Aimee Semple McPherson[3]

SPIRIT:
Feeling the "Nudge"

Is your life humdrum? Everything is going smoothly, no major conflicts week in and week out? There are times when God seems to bless and keep us from stress, but often those times are unexciting and routine. When you find yourself there, try this — study the leading of the Holy Spirit, and practice it!

A woman I admire called God's leading "the nudge of the Holy Spirit." We know we are led by the Holy Spirit, and that God's sheep (us) know God's voice.[1] But I marked her words because I had learned a very hard lesson about God's leading. Years before, I went for a few weeks without talking to my beloved mother. I had a distinct urge to call her, but shrugged it off — too busy, too expensive. After days of struggle, I received a call from my sister with the tragic words, "Mother died tonight." Why didn't I call when I felt the urge so strongly? It took some time for me to forgive myself for ignoring the "nudge."

Years later my sister and I felt "nudged" to make a long trip to visit an uncle we had not seen for decades. It was a blessed trip all around. When he died later, we were greatly satisfied that we were reacquainted with him.

Even at the most uneventful times, we must learn to stay attuned. I travel by airplane a lot, which becomes monotonous, but often I can share some of God's blessings with people seated next to me, whether saved or unsaved. There is something for everyone for blessing, healing, salvation. By following God's leading, you could save a marriage, a friendship, a life!

Have you been "nudged" to visit a neighbor? Or to hug your child as he trudged off to school? Or had a "nudge" thought about a relative whom you have not seen for a long time? Don't brush the thought aside thinking, "Oh, that's just me." Take the time to study, pray and obey, and you will find new joy as you are led by the Holy Spirit.

We never live uneventfully when we keep alive the readiness to be used of God wherever we go.

ACTION STEPS

* "Do it." Edwin says this all the time to well-meaning men who come to the altar to make a fresh start with the Lord or in their marriages. "Faith without works is dead,"[2] and there is nothing that substitutes for doing what you know in your heart is right. It may feel embarrassing the first time, but soon you will learn to set yourself aside and thrill to knowing you are used of God.

LET'S PRAY:

Father, help me to be sensitive to those many nudges of Your Holy Spirit. Help me to respond to those gentle "nudges;" give me the wisdom to know what to do in each case; and help me to be obedient. I thank You, Father, for leading me by Your Spirit. In Jesus' name I pray. Amen.

SHE SAID:

"God does not give women all those spiritual blessings to keep to themselves. He gives them to edify others, to enrich His Kingdom, and to accomplish His purposes through us."

— Nancy Corbett Cole[3]

HE SAID:

"Today's society puts a heavy burden on both men and women. Men feel the pressure to perform; women feel the pressure to conform . . . . God has an answer for that! God's answer is to please Him first and foremost. By pleasing God, a woman will be pleasing to others, including herself."

— Edwin Louis Cole[4]

WORTH QUOTING:

"The voice of God is always speaking to us, and always trying to get our attention. But His voice is a 'still, small voice,' and we must at least slow down in order to listen."
— Eugenia Price[5]

SUBMISSION:
The Road to Victory

Edwin and I pastored for several years and learned many valuable lessons. But just when we were becoming settled and secure, God led us back to the evangelistic field. Our finances dried up once again and my spirit seemed to wither with them. I felt God was working greatly through us — for everyone except us. As I tossed and turned one night, I recited Scriptures about how God meets our needs and, though weak, I tried to pray "in faith."

The next day, I was asked to sing at a church service. I was not surprised when God's Spirit impressed on me a certain song. I prepared it, thinking God was again planning wonderful things for others, while forgetting about me.

But in the meeting, as I sang "Submission," the words spoke to my own heart. God showed me how I was fighting circumstances in the flesh, not in the Spirit. My mind had almost convinced my heart that God had failed me, even though my heart kept crying out to Him. Tears sprang up as I sang, and in my spirit I began to yield. I sang so deeply in tune to God's Spirit that His Presence filled the auditorium and many people in the congregation met Him in a new way.

The meeting marked a turning point for me. Instead of wrestling through circumstances, I began to submit to God from deep within, trusting Him to work out the details of my life. And He did! I had thought it was enough to submit to my husband and the ministry God gave him, but my heart had been rebellious. Submitting outwardly just doesn't mean much unless we are submitted to God inwardly!

God's Word says to submit to Him, THEN resist the devil.[1] Once I submitted, I conquered some spiritual strongholds and our situation began to change — slowly.

We still had much to learn, but we were gaining ground. Submission to God was our road to victory!

ACTION STEPS

- Who or what are you struggling with? A boss, husband, circumstance? Instead of fighting with your will, surrender yourself to God in heartfelt prayer, then surrender the person or situation to Him. The Bible says that when we are weak, God makes us strong.[2] We have to surrender control and feel weak in our abilities in order to gain the presence of God's strength in our spirits.
- Submission means *far* more than the typical lessons we hear about wives submitting to husbands. That's only a few Scriptures among many, the most important of which deal with submitting to God. Edwin and I wrote a section on this topic in *The Unique Woman*. If you have not read this book, may I suggest that you do?
- "What is it to you what I do with someone else?" Jesus once asked Peter[3] (my paraphrase). Concentrate on doing what is right for you, and let God take care of others. When you submit to rightful authority (make sure it's rightful!), God will take care of you regardless of what others do. Ask God to reveal to you the many ways you benefit from a life that is fully submitted to Him. I'll name a few:
  - You submit to God's choice for a husband and are saved from years of unhappiness.
  - You submit to your pastor who makes a mistake that he learns from, resulting in a greatly matured minister.
  - You give your husband his way in something you disagree with, and learn new faith in God because your husband was actually right; or, because your husband chose wrongly but God took care of you anyway!
  - You submit when the department store clerk insists that you move to a longer line, and suddenly the item you have in your hand goes on sale.

A SONG:

1. *The path that I have trod,*
   Has brought me nearer to God,
   Tho' oft it led thro' sorrow's gates.
   Tho not the way I'd choose,
   In my way I might lose
   The joy that yet for me awaits.
2. *Submission to the will*
   Of Him Who guides me still
   Is surety of His love revealed:
   My soul shall rise above
   This world in which I move;
   I conquer only where I yield.

                                    — Mrs. R. R. Forman[4]

SHE SAID:

"Submission is a great tool for character building. God tests the faith of men and women as He calls them to submit themselves to His divine commands."

— Nancy Corbett Cole[5]

HE SAID:

"Submission is God's method of revealing His 'transcendent glory' in the restoration process. His transcendent glory is His ability to take things meant for evil and convert them to work for our good, when they are submitted and committed to Him."

— Edwin Louis Cole[6]

LET'S PRAY:

Father, teach me to submit to You, trusting You to work things out in my favor. Help me to understand Your divine system of authority. Then help me to respect the position of those who hold authority over me, realizing that You are still over them. Please forgive my heart's rebellion. As I submit to You, I now resist the devil's attacks against me and my family. We are shielded through faith in Jesus. I thank You, God, for You are putting me on the road to victory and I accept Your work in my life. Through Your Son Jesus I pray. Amen.

PRAYER:
Take Up a Sword!

Have you ever encountered a woman who is spiritual dynamite? One person like that is my friend, Janey. She is so quiet, unassuming, petite and pretty, that you would not think of her as a powerful woman, but when she prays you know all heaven listens.

A major difference between Janey and many other women is that she is convinced God is listening to and answering every prayer. She prays fervently for His Will to be accomplished in her life and the lives of her family. She goes to battle in prayer against Satan's evil forces that would harm them.

The Bible tells us we are warriors. A warrior is defined as one who fights battles. Deborah was a judge in Israel and also a warrior. When Barak went to battle for the Israelites, he insisted that Deborah go with him to help him win.[1] She went and the Israelites were victorious.

We can be victorious warriors for the Lord, too   not in a physical sense, as Deborah was, but in a spiritual sense like Janey — through prayer and intercession for others.

The Bible says, "The kingdom of heaven suffereth violence, and the violent take it by force."[2] This means we hold onto the promises of God and never let go. We strive for what we believe God wants for us, our loved ones, our nation, and anyone or any place in the world that grips our heart.

When Deborah won the battle over the Canaanites, she had a song to sing. We can sing, too, when we become warriors in prayer and win battles over evil.

ACTION STEPS
* Start considering yourself a warrior for God. Read Ephesians 6:13-17 out loud, personalizing each verse as you put on the spiritual armor of God.

- Make a list of people and concerns. Then make a date with yourself to take some time all alone. Start by praising God, then pray until you receive peace about every item on your prayer list.
- Take time every day to pray, even if it is only five minutes at first.
- Make appointments between yourself and God as airtight as a trip to the beauty salon so that you keep them. Spending two hours one time with God will spur you to want to do it more often!

SHE SAID:

"Women who refuse to be spiritual overcomers get overcome by others."
— Nancy Corbett Cole[3]

HE SAID:

"I learned the 'principles of intercession' from an internationally known teacher, Joy Dawson. She taught me things about prayer that I had never known, and she challenged me to practice them. The deep intimacy Nancy and I now have came from applying those principles. They changed my life and my marriage. When we practiced them together, it brought us an intimacy and unity that I never dreamed possible."
— Edwin Louis Cole[4]

NINE KEYS TO EFFECTIVE INTERCESSION:[5]

1. CONFESS ALL KNOWN SIN FROM YOUR LIFE. You cannot harbor sin and still be effective in intercessory prayer. Sin only comes out of your life by way of your mouth. Forgiveness brings release from those things God reveals to you.
   Psalm 6:18; 1 John 1:9
2. ACKNOWLEDGE YOUR NEED OF THE HOLY SPIRIT TO DIRECT YOUR PRAYER. Effective prayer is energized by the Spirit of God within you. Allow the Holy Spirit to bring to your mind the things which are in agreement with God and His will.
   Romans 8:26
3. DIE TO YOUR OWN DESIRES, IMAGINATIONS AND PRAYER BURDENS. Discipline your prayer time from interruptions and rampant thoughts. Focus on being in the presence of God. He will speak to you in the Word and in the Spirit.
   Proverbs 3:5,6; Isaiah 55:8
4. ASK GOD TO FILL YOU COMPLETELY WITH HIS HOLY SPIRIT. Receive the fullness of the Spirit in faith. The infilling of His Spirit produces the opportunity for Him to control your prayer thoughts.
   Ephesians 5:18
5. PRAISE GOD IN FAITH FOR THE PRAYER TIME YOU ARE ABOUT TO EXPERIENCE. God works in our lives consistent with His character. He desires to elevate us to His level

of faith. Praise and faith work hand-in-hand to bring to reality answers to prayer.
Psalm 100:4

6. DEAL AGGRESSIVELY WITH THE ENEMY. Our resistance to the enemy is proportionate to our submission to the Lord. Do not be intimidated by Satan's temptations or accusations. Be impressed with the power that God's righteousness produces in us.
James 4:7

7. WAIT IN SILENT EXPECTANCY FOR WHAT GOD BRINGS TO YOUR MIND. Pray verbally, believing God for His wisdom and direction to guide you. Do not move to the next subject until you are sure God has discharged all He desires to reveal in a specific area.
John 10:27

8. CONFIRM PRAYER WITH THE WORD. Use your Bible to reference the direction God gives you in prayer. Keep a notebook to record the things God speaks to you.
Psalm 119:105

9. PRAISE GOD FOR HIS MARVELOUS WORK IN YOUR LIFE. God answers prayer! He rewards those who diligently seek Him. He is worthy of praise for who He is and what He does in our lives.
Romans 11:36

QUOTABLE:

" 'Twas God the word that spake it,
He took the Bread and brake it;
And what the word did make it,
That I believe, and take it."

— *Queen Elizabeth I*[6]

"Mine eyes have seen the glory of the coming of the Lord . . . His truth is marching on."
— *Julia Ward Howe*[7]
(1819-1910)

"Deep inside your heart, begin to believe a daring truth: God doesn't want you to lead a mediocre life."
— *Anne Ortlund*[8]

FOUR

WEAVING RELATION- SHIPS

FRIENDS:
Recognize True Friendship

My daughter went to her counsellor at school one day because she was troubled about several of her friends. She told him how some of them seemed to be using her for their own advantage, and others seemed to drain the life out of her. She expected the counsellor to sympathize with her and give her some insight into these people. Instead he asked, "Why do you only have these types of friendships? Do you always have to be a rescuer or confessor?" This was a wise man! He made my daughter search out what a real friend is.

We do not need to drop relationships with those who continually need help, but we do need to recognize the difference between those and true friendships that are mutually rewarding. True friendship is a sharing of common ideals and interests, a bond that can grow from working together, going to school, or being in the same church group. Friends mutually support each other and are genuinely concerned for the other's welfare. Friendships demand loyalty, honesty, sharing of strengths and weaknesses, and never betraying confidences.

It is often said that familiarity breeds contempt, but this is not so in friendships. There is no contempt when weaknesses are known, but instead they become opportunities to pray together, realizing that what befalls one could easily befall the other.

Make friends, those who improve and enhance your life. Recognize the women who need counsel only. Love, appreciate and minister to them, but recognize the difference between them and your intimate friends. This will give you great peace of mind.

Jesus is a friend who sticks "closer than a brother."[1] He is our model for friendship. As we try to be Christlike in friendship, realize that a Christlike friend is far better than friends with wealth, beauty or status.

ACTION STEPS

* Take inventory of your friendships. Whom do you trust and depend on? Whom do you draw close to simply because they are popular, wealthy or have something you desire? And who is a drain on you, constantly needing help? Prayerfully bring them before the Lord and differentiate who is ministering to whom, and with whom you are on an equal footing.
* Set limits to the relationships that drain you. Let them know you can only talk on the phone for xx minutes, or that you do not accept calls after a certain hour.
* The Bible says to "show yourself friendly." Learn a friendly manner, regardless of how shy you are or how hurt you have been in previous friendships. Once you are showing a friendly face, trust God to bring friends into your life that return your friendship.
* If possible, make your husband your best friend!

SIX WAYS TO MAKE PEOPLE LIKE YOU:[2]
by Dale Carnegie

1. Become genuinely interested in other people.
2. Smile.
3. Remember that a person's name is to that person the sweetest and most important sound in any language.
4. Be a good listener. Encourage others to talk about themselves.
5. Talk in terms of the other person's interest.
6. Make the other person feel important — and do it sincerely.

FOOD FOR THOUGHT:

"For there is no friend like a sister
In calm or stormy weather."
— *Christina Georgina Rossetti*[3]

GOOD TIMES:
You Don't Have To Feel Neglected

Have you ever heard anyone say, "No one remembered my birthday"? People who do not speak up until it is too late leave those around them uncomfortable and often feeling guilty.

Amy was one of a group of women I worked with who exuded self-confidence. Once she came into work with a package under her arm. "What's that?" we asked. "Today is my birthday," she said, "and I wanted to celebrate it with you." With that she tore open the paper and revealed a delicious assortment of cookies which we happily munched all day. Her unabashed assertiveness taught me not to wait for others either to notice or neglect me, but to take things into my own hands. She helped me overcome the risk of getting the hurt feelings from being left out by illustrating to me that I need to use my voice.

How many times has someone said to you, "I'm not a mindreader. Tell me what's on your mind." When the words finally spill out, we often find that misunderstandings clear up and relationships deepen. We need to shun accusations and self-pity to speak with truthful sincerity. Laziness, insecurity and pride often keep us from revealing our thoughts. We need to rise up and speak! Make a resolve to speak out at the right time and in the right spirit today. Do you need to resolve something? Don't wait for the other person to ask, "What's wrong?" Pray about it, tell them, pray with them if you can, then move on! Are you rejoicing about something today? Take those cookies to work and share your happiness with others.

ACTION STEPS
* Don't set people up to fail! Let your mate or your friends know when your anniversary

or birthday is. If they forget to ask you about an important event in your life, tell them anyway!

• Put up a large calendar in your kitchen, bathroom, or wherever your husband or family can see it. Mark clearly all birthdays and anniversaries.

• God never neglects you, so celebrate! Think of reasons to make today a special day, then do something appropriate with someone you love.

WORTH QUOTING:

"Laugh, and the world laughs with you;
Weep, and you weep alone."

— *Ella Wheeler Wilcox*[1]
(1850-1919)

"Share your accomplishments with your child. The more your child senses that you value yourself, the greater the value your child will place upon you. And the greater he will value your expressions of love."

— *Jan Dargatz*[2]

CHILDLESSNESS:
God's Plans and Ours

There are many women who do not have children, yet yearn every day to be called "mother." Maybe you have looked forward to the day when you would become a mother, and yet for whatever reason it has never come.

A friend named Tara was married seven years before her first child was born. She became disheartened, resentful, frustrated, and felt as though she was a "neuter." Month after month she faced her childlessness, while her friends had one, then two, and some even three babies.

Heartsick and frustrated as she started her seventh year of marriage, Tara cried out a key prayer to God: "What is Your plan for my life?" God faithfully gave her some scriptures that filled her with hope for a year of blessing for her and her husband, Bill. When Bill suddenly lost his job and they experienced other setbacks, she wondered if she really had heard from God. But she kept praying and one by one, things started falling into place.

A momentous time came a few months later when, without being tested, Tara had a feeling that she was pregnant. She had imagined such feelings before, and even though this seemed real, it took her two months to get up enough courage to go to a doctor. He confirmed her feeling, and within months, she and Bill were rejoicing in their beautiful firstborn.

God revealed to Tara before giving her the child that she and Bill were too immature to have children when they first wanted them. He told her He was sovereign and does all things for our good. When she finally asked for His plans, instead of begging for her plans, He told her to set her spiritual house in order, and press into Him in prayer to receive all He had for her.

Hannah in the Bible endured insults from her husband's other wife until she finally asked God specifically for a baby.[1] God wants to give us the desires of our hearts, but He wants us to ask specifically for them from a heart that is fully yielded to Him. Hannah gave her first child, Samuel, to the Lord. Then God gave her five other children to fill her house with the sound of childish laughter, song and running feet.[2]

How we appreciate God's move in our lives after we have come to the end, and thrown ourselves at His feet, acknowledging our total dependence on Him! God loves to give us the desires of our hearts that He has authored, as we press into Him in prayer.

ACTION STEPS
* If you are childless, not through your own choosing, find God's promises for YOU and stand on them. Press in to God in prayer. Meditate upon His Word, stay in an expectant attitude with your spiritual ears open to His voice, and obey whatever He says.
* Childlessness is one of the most delicate areas in a woman's life. When people say insensitive things to you, usually out of ignorance to your plight, just keep in mind who you are in Christ. You must stay ''on top'' spiritually, knowing that you are who and where God wants you to be in order to ward off the expectations and comments of others.
* Often the newly married woman's plight is for others to switch from ''When are you going to get married?'' to ''When are you going to have children?'' If you are tempted to ask someone or if someone asks you about having children, remember what Miss Manners says: No one has the right to ask about the state of anyone's womb! That is their personal territory, not to be invaded by others. Her suggested response is a frozen smile and silence.

THINK ABOUT IT:
"He settles the barren woman in her home as a happy mother of children."
     — *Psalm 113:9 NIV*

"May he give you the desire of your heart and make all your plans succeed."
     — *Psalm 20:4 NIV*

"You have granted him the desire of his heart and have not withheld the request of his lips."
     — *Psalm 21:2 NIV*

MOMS:
Making Moments Count

"**M**om, I can't find my Math book!"
"Mom, can you help me with this blouse?"
"Mom, Robby spilled his cereal."
So goes the morning of the single mom. There is no let-up and no one will help. If she has an outside job with its demands as well, every day becomes a struggle. Evenings are dinner, clothes, baths, homework, and prayers. Weekends mean grocery shopping, cleaning, and appointments. Sundays provide a time of spiritual nourishment that carries Mom through the week . . . once she gets the family to church.

If this is your life, take heart — it doesn't last forever! Children do grow up, so try to make your time with them a treasure instead of a pressure.

My friend, Adair, raised two sons as a single parent and worked as a busy executive. One day the children seemed like such a pressure that she dreaded going home. About 4 p.m. that afternoon, she called her oldest and said she would be home late. She told him where the food was and to make sure his younger brother ate dinner. After work, she treated herself to a meal and some shopping. When she returned home, the boys had eaten uneventfully and were calmly talking on the phone and playing. Suddenly she realized how much she pressured herself to take care of them, instead of simply enjoying them.

We can relieve a lot of pressure with good communication. When you are frustrated or lonely, don't take it out on your children. Instead, communicate that it's time for Mom to take a break. Ask small ones to do something special for you. Speak frankly to teens and request that they do some chore while you go out to read the newspaper at a coffee shop.

101

We can also be prepared! Read a good book or article on child development and identify where your children are. If you'll invest some time on this, it will put you one valuable step ahead of them.

And, pray faithfully for your children! God is answering your prayer according to His faithfulness, regardless of how you may feel. It's best to talk to God about your children before you talk to them directly. You may think your work in raising your children will never end, but it does! Soon they will start leaving home, one by one. Make every moment now count as one to cherish.

SINGLE MOMS:

*   If you have sons without a father, try to find a father figure, perhaps from church, scouts or sports, who will take an interest in them.

*   My husband has some excellent material you could use to teach your sons about manhood. Ask your bookstore for *Courage,* or other books by Edwin Louis Cole.

*   Find a support group of single parents, or any parents, to share problems, advice, and ideas. As you hear others' experiences in raising children, you may find yours are not so different after all. This relieves pressure.

ALL MOMS:

*   Watch the newspapers for problems that may be at your child's school. Go to the school's open house to meet their teachers, and let the teachers know someone cares about your child.

*   Watch for any signs that your child may be having trouble academically or socially. Any deviation from his or her normal routine may warrant investigation.

*   If you cannot find or afford a responsible baby sitter, trade sitting dates with another mother to take some free time for yourself. A few hours away from the kids can make you feel like a new person.

*   To stay ahead of everyone, schedule "family council" meetings regularly, once a week if possible.

— Let the children voice their concerns, and allow yourself to voice yours as well. If you know you get to lay your feelings out in the open once a week, it is much easier to stay calm during frustrating times. This is true for the child as well, and reinforces that he/she is an important member of the family who is taken seriously.

— Ask each child frankly about privileges and disciplines administered during the last week. You will avoid resentment on their part by letting them discuss any unfairness they perceived — real or imagined.

— Go over the family calendar. Just discussing upcoming events can encourage a sluggish memory or timid heart to speak up about joining some activity or sport.

— End with devotions. If you do not have a regular devotional schedule, read the Proverb for the day (there are 31 chapters in Proverbs, and 31 days of the month), and have prayer.

- Try what some successful mothers do: take each child separately into your bedroom (three times a year is plenty, perhaps just after school starts, over the holidays, and again at Spring Break). Ask them how they are doing socially, economically, academically, emotionally, physically, and at home, stopping after each subject to ask specifically, *"How can I help you?"* Ask their opinion, *"Am I doing the right things for you?"* When you express this attention and willingness to be on their side, it is amazing how they come out with their deepest fears about a physical flaw, or their unspoken desire to have a new bedspread, or a problem they are having with a teacher, or the fact that a friend got them to try drugs!

SOMETHING TO THINK ABOUT:

In 1965 the average parent spent 30 hours a week with a child. Today the average parent spends only 17 hours.[1]

FAMILY MATTERS:

When Mother Theresa received her Nobel Prize, she was asked, "What can we do to promote world peace?" She replied, "Go home and love your family."[2]

WORTH QUOTING:

"[Daddy] said: 'All children must look after their own upbringing.' Parents can only give good advice or put them on the right paths, but the final forming of a person's character lies in their own hands."

— Anne Frank[3]
(1929-1945)

"Who ran to me when I fell,
And would some pretty story tell,
Or kiss the place to make it well?
My mother."

— Ann Taylor[4]
(1782-1866)

"Death and taxes and childbirth! There's never any convenient time for any of them."
— Margaret Mitchell[5]
(1900-1949)

"By and large, mothers and housewives are the only workers who do not have regular time off."
— Anne Morrow Lindbergh[6]

CHILDREN:
Raise Them for the Lord

When I became a mother, I made my biggest priority to be a good wife, to provide my children first and foremost with a peaceful home. But my second priority was to pour my heart into motherhood! When I set eyes on my first child, Paul, bundled in hospital blankets, my heart swelled, my eyes teared up and a thrill went through me. The thrill has never left. I love motherhood!

Good mothering meant seeing to the physical needs of my children, that they were fed the proper foods and dressed adequately and appropriately. But the greater challenge that has lasted through the years is spiritual parenting.

My youngest, Joann, seemed a model child. Her sister, Lois, called her "Miss Perfect." Paul and Lois forged through the teenage years, and I thought most of my work was done. But then Joann hit those adolescent years and made up for all the things she'd never done before! I then recognized that of everything I did, her spiritual welfare was the most important thing to ensure.

Our children's spiritual well-being is a parental concern that never diminishes. Children's choices of lifetime mates, their career choices and all their plans begin with their choice to follow God wholeheartedly.

Dozens of women over the years have told me with choked up voices that they wish they could start over, that their children are making deplorable choices and are "nowhere" with God. My heart goes out to the well-intentioned parents who thought they did everything right, only to have it blow up in their faces. It is truly discouraging.

While meditating on this one day, God showed me ten practical ways a mother can help her child's spiritual welfare. Prayerfully consider these listed below. Whatever you do, avoid a contest of wills. Set the rules, set the consequences for obeying or breaking the rules, then quietly follow through. Pointing out their failings just distracts them from learning about the naturally negative consequences that follow poor behavior.

All three of my children love the Lord today, and I can attest to the countless hours of prayer that go into each one. Being a good parent takes a lot of effort! But think of the rewards: Healthy, happy and confident children; godly citizens who make good choices; your own joy in watching your children develop.

ACTION STEPS

- *Keep a godly atmosphere in your home.* Be a living example, not one who says, "Do as I say, not as I do." Pray for and with the children.
- *Never miss church.* Unless it is humanly impossible to go, be there. This instills reverence for God and for His House.
- *Never disagree with your husband in front of your children.* Difficult to accomplish, but a great way to practice diplomatic discussion.
- *Refrain from gossip of all kinds.* Never talk about fellow believers in front of your children. Hypocrisy turns children off. If you want your children to respect you, live a life that is worthy of respect. They will learn to love and respect both you and the God you represent.
- *Maintain family devotions.* At some time of the day when the family is together, have devotions. You can use the time together for planning as well, which provides security.
- *Know the young man or woman your child is dating.* Set realistic guidelines on where they can go, with whom, and a curfew. Even when children are adults, if they are living under your roof, you have the right and responsibility to look after their well-being.
- *Give children latitude.* Just because someone else dresses a certain way, do not make your children conform to that image. Straight hair was the style when my daughters were in high school, and I actually helped one of my daughters iron the natural wave out of her hair every morning before school! This was certainly not my taste, but it was also not immodest or rebellious and so I didn't impose my will on hers.
- *Invite godly people to your home.* Bring someone into your home that has the touch of heaven on them and your children will take notice. The person may say the same thing you've been saying, but now your children hear and are impressed. (Make sure you don't say, "That's what I've said all along." Pride gets you nowhere.)
- *Forgive your children daily.* They may embarass you, shock you, humiliate you, but don't hold it against them. They are unconscious of this most of the time.
- *Know what your children watch on television.* Children watch an average of twenty-two hours of television weekly. Many cartoons and teenaged situation comedies introduce the occult, violence and sexual situations. Watching television with your children could be an eye-opener for you. When a program is below your standards, discuss it openly with them. Get their reactions and give them yours, not to condemn but to help in setting

standards. (We need to be flexible, not condemning.) Set loving, realistic boundaries. Plan with them what they will watch; good sitcoms and cartoons as well as nature, history and cultural programs. Help them develop creative alternatives, such as reading and hobbies. Set an example by doing the same.

PRAY GOD'S WORD:

Here are a few of the many great Scriptures you can pray over your children:

". . . I [the Lord] will fight those who fight you, and I will save your children."
— Isaiah 49:25 TLB

"All your children shall be taught by the Lord, and great shall be the peace of your children."
— Isaiah 54:13 NKJV

". . . I will pour My Spirit on your descendants, and My blessing on your offspring; They will spring up among the grass like willows by the watercourses."
— Isaiah 44:3,4 NKJV

"There is hope for your future, says the Lord, and your children will come again to their own land."
— Jeremiah 31:17 TLB

QUOTABLE QUOTES:

"A mother is not a person to lean on, but a person to make leaning unnecessary."
— Dorothy Canfield Fisher[1]
(1879-1958)

"The children could not go without me. I could not possibly leave the King, and the King would never leave."
— Elizabeth,
the Queen Mother of England,[2]
reported replying as to whether
the princesses would leave England
after the bombing of Buckingham
Palace during World War II

CHRISTIAN EDUCATION:
Proper Dress for War

A couple I know maintained that if they prayed with their children at night and took them to one church service on Sunday, they did not really need any other Christian training. One day this mother was part of a group I was with, and her children were playing with some of the others. Suddenly her ten-year-old daughter rushed into the room and asked excitedly, "Mom, who's Moses?"

Her mother's excruciating embarrassment was covered by others who explained to the little girl who the great man of God was. The innocent, childish question spoke volumes to the mother who soon had a Christian training program started. Children must be trained in the way they should go and it will stick with them for life.[1]

After becoming a Christian, I attended Sunday School regularly with my children. Each evening we had "family altar" where we read from the Bible and prayed, and at the evening meal we recited a Scripture before saying grace. Our church had training programs for boys and girls during the mid-week service where my children memorized large portions of Scripture. By these means, the Word was lodged deeply into all of our hearts.

The Bible tells us to put on the whole armor of God, which includes faith, righteousness, salvation, peace, truth, and the power of the Holy Spirit.[2] It is an apt description, for what soldier could expect to win without knowing what every piece of the battle outfit meant? How foolish it would be to go to war improperly dressed or without understanding of the equipment. Yet many of us have not provided for indoctrination into the Word of God, which is the only way to become properly attired with the armour of God.[3]

My children are now teaching their children. Last summer my son, Paul, took his sons to a Christian camp in Oklahoma. While driving home to Texas, Paul announced, "Look boys, we're crossing the famous Red River." Nine-year-old Bryce looked around and, full of what he had just learned in camp, mistook the Red River for the Red Sea.

"Dad," he asked soberly. "Did Egypt used to be in Oklahoma?"

While misunderstanding Bible geography will not harm you, there is also no reason to live on a nine-year-old level forever! Take seriously the spiritual war we are in! It is not against flesh and blood or personalities, but it is against spiritual forces that we must be armed to fight.

ACTION STEPS
* Take yourself and your children to church at every opportunity. Our church had a scouting program for boys that merged physical with spiritual training and was highly effective. The girls learned sports, missions work, and the Bible. If your church does not have something for both boys and girls, perhaps you could get your pastor's blessing to start something. There are plenty of resources available.
* Take on a project to further your own understanding of Scripture. Memorize the books of the Bible, the basic salvation Scriptures, the great passages such as the "armor of God" in Ephesians 6:10-18.
* Begin reading the Bible systematically. I really like my "One Year Bible" in the Living translation, but there are many yearly reading programs that are terrific.
* Start a study program for yourself, perhaps with studies on "salvation," "prayer," and other key words.
* Pick up those little commentaries that go through one book of the Bible at a time and begin working through them. You will be surprised at how far you can get with just seven to ten minutes per night. And it is so interesting, soon you will go to bed early, or put the kids down early, just to spend more time with it!

SCRIPTURES TO MEMORIZE:

'For God so loved the world, that he gave his only begotten Son, that whosoever believeth in him should not perish, but have everlasting life."
                                                            — John 3:16

"For the wages of sin is death; but the gift of God is eternal life through Jesus Christ our Lord."

                                                            — Romans 6:23

"For all have sinned, and come short of the glory of God."
— Romans 3:23

"Jesus answered and said unto him, Verily, verily, I say unto thee, Except a man be born again, he cannot see the kingdom of God."
— John 3:3

"If we confess our sins, he is faithful and just to forgive us our sins, and to cleanse us from all unrighteousness."
— 1 John 1:9

"That if thou shalt confess with thy mouth the Lord Jesus, and shalt believe in thine heart that God hath raised him from the dead, thou shalt be saved.
"For with the heart man believeth unto righteousness; and with the mouth confession is made unto salvation."
— Romans 10:9,10

"And they said, Believe on the Lord Jesus Christ, and thou shalt be saved, and thy house."
— Acts 16:31

WORTH QUOTING:

"Learning is not attained by chance, it must be sought for with ardor and attended to with diligence."

— *Abigail Adams*[4]
(1744-1818)

"I was never allowed to read the popular American children's books of my day because, as my mother said, the children spoke bad English without the author's knowing it."
— *Edith Wharton*[5]
(1862-1937)

"The teaching that the Bible is a myth, is just as dogmatic, after all, as the dogmatic teaching of it as history."
— *Edith Schaeffer*[6]

"Now I believe that the Bible is, to the spiritual life of a Christian, what warm fresh whole wheat bread is to the physical life — both nourishing and appetising [sic]!"
— *Edith Schaeffer*[7]

DELEGATE:
Improve Your Life

My daughter called recently and put my granddaughter, Kendal, on the phone. I could hear Lois saying, "Kendal, tell Grandma what you did today." Kendal very proudly told me how she folded the clean clothes and helped with the dinner dishes. What a wise daughter I have!

Small children like six-year-old Kendal generally want to help Mommy do things around the house. Often we say, "No dear, you're too little. Wait until you're older," not realizing that the best time to train is when the child is eager to learn.

When they are older, we often can hardly tolerate the way they do things. We tell them to never mind, we'll do the job ourselves. Then we discover we're worn out, overtired and resentful of all the tasks we have to do. Not to mention we are raising children who don't know how to do anything and feel they do not significantly contribute to the family.

Try a word of praise for every new task a child accomplishes. Even if our teenager runs an entire washer cycle with just one sweatshirt in it, at least he or she is showing the initiative to run the washer! New skills can always be added, once the child is going in the right direction.

This carries over into the church also. Instead of delegating responsibility, we often try to do it all ourselves — singing, leading the choir, heading the women's ministries, overseeing food functions or helping the poor and needy. After a while, we grow resentful and wonder, "Where is everyone else?" We may not remember all the times people said, "Can I help?" but we thought at the moment that we could do the job alone better. The treadmill of overwork taxes not only us but our families, as time grows short and tempers also.

When you have the authority, get all the help you need to get the job done, and use everyone who says they will help. Even if they cannot cook, they can sit by the phone to prevent distractions while you and others do the cooking! Others, especially your children, may not do as perfect a job as you would, but they might surprise you by doing a better job — if not the first time, then when you have trained them!

ACTION STEPS

* Remember that involving others frees you to do other things (or rest!), enables the job to be completed more efficiently, and brings otherwise disparate people together to accomplish something — a veritable hotbed for growing friendships.
* Be creative about your activities. Is there a way to involve others? Is there a way to meet others by involving them? If so, pick up the phone and start delegating and involving!
* What is happening at your house? Is it your husband who doesn't help? Ask him to help in a new way that is not nagging — how about if he cooks the dinner or goes shopping with the children while you finish a project that he traditionally would do?
* Determine that the next time anyone — from church, work, or family — says they will help you do something, you will say "yes" first. Then you can think up a way they can help!
* Here are some ideas:
  — Sunday School teachers — ask members or parents to do small, specific jobs for your class or next social.
  — Bible study leaders — put people in charge of follow-up, setting up the room, bringing refreshments.
  — Office workers — teach a subordinate how to do something you assumed you needed to do. Even if you help and check their work, this could eventually free you to do "extras" and position you for a promotion!
  — Mothers — give your two year old a cloth and let him copy you as you dust; put your twelve year old in charge of the whole dinner; let everyone try a job traditionally done by you or someone else (such as cleaning baseboards or doing laundry).
  — Wives — when your husband volunteers to help, let him! Have you pushed him aside to take over when he fumbled to make a sandwich? Or said, "No, I'll do it," when he offered to help with the children. You're not always helping him; you're sometimes cutting him off!
* Delegate, delegate, delegate!

WORTH QUOTING:

"I slept and dreamed that life was beauty.
I woke — and found that life was duty."
　　　　　　　　　　　　　— *Ellen Sturgis Hooper*[1]
　　　　　　　　　　　　　(1816-1841)

I LOVE YOU:
Words of Life

I was getting my newspaper from the driveway this morning when my neighbor's son left for school. *"Love you, Mom,"* he said as he ran off with his friends. It was heartwarming just to hear. Three little words, *"I love you,"* are the words that topple empires, shape destinies, make men and women risk their lives and unite millions of couples in holy matrimony every year. What power is in those words!

We can never say "I love you" too often. In an old story a wife complained to her husband, "You never tell me you love me." He replied, "I told you when I married you that I loved you. If it ever changes, I'll let you know." It makes for a good joke, but not a good marriage.

Some people think if they say "I love you," they will look weak or lose authority. Untrue! When you say "I love you," you renew commitment and build bonds. Love is the mortar between the bricks of experience that builds relationships.

My friend, Gayle, had a rebellious teenaged son. As she prayed for him, the Holy Spirit impressed her just to say "I love you." Before he left for school and first thing when he came home, she looked him straight in the eyes and said, "Dave, I love you." There was no immediate change, but as months passed and he matured, his heart turned toward Gayle. They weathered a difficult situation, and came out loving more.

There are times when we feel less than loving. We might want to speak sharply or not at all. Saying, "I love you," paves the way for forgiveness — forgiving others, or them forgiving you. Jesus went to the cross because of love. On the cross He released us by saying, "Father, forgive them."[1] He died so we could live; He forgave so we could be forgiven and forgive others; He loved so we could freely say, "I love you."

ACTION STEPS
* When was the last time a loved one had a day filled with rejection, disappointment

or failure? How comforting for them to hear someone say, "I love you." Did you say it or show it? Try it out the next time.

- Say "I love you" often. You may do something for your husband, children, or another loved one and they may feel your love, but it makes a tremendous difference to turn to them and say, "I am doing this because I love you."
- Words are confirmed by actions. Try something along these lines: Pick up a jar of apple sauce today for your youngest who loves it, or a pack of baseball cards or gum for each child. Give it to the child and say, "I love you." He also will hear, "I know you, I know what you like, and I love you enough to provide it." Wow! What an impact! And it cost less than a dollar with a nice thought.

LET'S PRAY:

Father, I thank You for Your unconditional love. Thank You, Lord, that the love of Christ is shed abroad in my heart. I choose to love, Father. Help me to love not just those who are easy to love, my friends and my family, but also to love the unlovely. Help me to be thoughtful and sensitive to the needs of others. Help me to become a vessel for Your love to be poured into; then let that love continually overflow into the lives of others.
In Jesus' name I pray Amen.

LOVE'S CHECKLIST:

"Love is patient, love is kind. It does not envy, it does not boast, it is not proud. It is not rude, it is not self-seeking, it is not easily angered, it keeps no record of wrongs. Love does not delight in evil but rejoices with the truth. It always protects, always trusts, always hopes, always perseveres. Love never fails . . . ."
— 1 Corinthians 13:4-8a NIV

"Let love be your greatest aim . . . . "
— 1 Corinthians 14:1a TLB

". . . Love one another."
— John 13:34b NIV

WORTH QUOTING:

"How do I love thee? Let me count the ways."
— *Elizabeth Barrett Browning*[2]

"We can consider ourselves a Loved Person, not because of our circumstances or situations but simply because God loves us perfectly, totally and eternally."
— *Marie Chapian*[3]

"Though God hath raised me high, yet this I count the glory of my crown: that I have reigned with your loves."

— *Queen Elizabeth I*[4]
(1533-1603)

PASTOR'S WIFE:
Gracious Help

The speed of life seems to increase a notch each hour during the Christmas season. Time and allegiances are divided between home, church, work, and the extended family. This December morning at 7:45 a pastor called my husband's hotel from his home in an earlier time zone. He had prayed, exercised, dressed, driven to the office, gone through his mail and it was still only 5:45 a.m. where he was! When I think of all I attempted when I was a pastor's wife, I don't know how I accomplished anything.

One year, during the Christmas season, I was also working at a secular job with a one-hour commute each way to work. I was in the choir's cantata, hosted back-to-back dinners for the staff and board in my home, attended almost every party and banquet and, as head of women's ministries, organized the year-end outreaches and celebrations. I loved doing God's work, but I must admit I felt quite exhausted at times!

We tend to expect pastor's wives to do the types of things I did while staying well-groomed, loving and gracious to all, never late for anything, and toting delicious dishes to every potluck. She may well have her own children's band recitals, class parties, school plays, or Girl Scouts activities as well. Every child's program has rehearsals, and she may also have house guests. Then when those late night emergency calls come, she must drop all priorities to take care of the flock, and her husband.

Most pastor's wives do all this without benefit of a secretary or housekeeper, and with no remuneration.

This is a rather elaborate reminder for all of us to appreciate our own pastor's wife. No one but God ever knows all she is going through, nor is she at liberty to divulge it. Instead of criticizing her, we honor her, respect her in the position God has given her, and pray for her. Most pastor's wives are never trained for the position. It was only in Edwin's last pastorate that I finally felt comfortable in that role for the first time. Thank

God for all the gracious people who overlooked my flaws over the years. Be a gracious person, be a blessing, and you will endear yourself to many a valiant pastor's wife.

ACTION STEPS
* Pray daily for your pastor and his family. As God's anointed leaders, they are constantly antagonized by the enemies of God.
* When you invite your pastor's wife to do anything, think ahead of how it can be a blessing, not a burden to her.
* If you invite her to do something without children, offer to pay for a babysitter. If it's a group function, secretly collect a few dollars from each participant to cover it. (Babysitting costs alone can strain a young pastor's budget, and older siblings expected to take up the slack could become resentful.)
* If you invite her to a potluck, relieve her from the responsibility to cook for it. Make sure there is plenty without burdening her.
* Ask her far in advance to attend any activity so she has time to clear her calendar, and compare calendars with her husband. This literally takes hours each month to plan and synchronize!
* If you invite her and she cancels for any reason, don't take it personally! Remember, if there is an emergency, she is not always at liberty to discuss it.
* Give her permission to say "no" without guilt.
* If your pastor's wife is unpaid like most, give gifts from time to time to give her that much-needed sense of worth. Sometimes a gift certificate from her favorite store is most welcome, and takes the pressure off you to guess the best gift.
* Think of ways to help during the holidays. Could you take her children for an evening while she goes to a party? If you cook, perhaps you could help her entertain by cooking at home (not at her house!), and just dropping off a dish or cake with her. If your children are in the church play with hers, maybe you could pick hers up on the way to rehearsals. Remember, you will have to offer your services. One of the unspoken expectations of her is to do everything without asking for help.
* Never criticize your pastor's wife, not to your husband or anyone. Get out all the negative when you are alone with God and ask Him to take care of it. He may change her — or He may change you. Stay open!

SOMETHING TO THINK ABOUT:
"The most exhausting thing in life is being insincere."
— *Anne Morrow Lindbergh*[1]

IN-LAWS:
Rewards of Preseverance

A long with repeating vows and becoming one with your husband when you marry, you also become part of another family. Most of us discover differences in this relationship. Some in-laws are openly critical of their child's spouse, and others view them as competition. And some spouses are jealous of the in-laws.

A man wrote me and my husband about his situation. Sam's parents never opened their home to his bride. Fearing their disapproval, he visited them without her. In time, his parents' attitudes influenced him to treat his wife with disrespect, too. Difficult years passed until one day the Lord convicted Sam of neglecting his wife. Sam repented, then tearfully apologized to his wife and son.

They went together to his parents' house where he told them of his change of heart toward his wife. Sam announced that he would no longer visit without her. It was a dramatic beginning to a restored marriage. By the way, within months the whole family accepted Sam's wife.

There are always two sides to every relationship. Often there are expectations and attitudes coming from the other side that we cannot control. But we can always control ourselves. We choose whether to be open to the Lord, forgiving and loving, or spiteful, resentful and angry. And we choose whether or not we will place the situation in the Lord's hands through serious prayer.

My mother-in-law and I are very close and love each other dearly, but it wasn't always so. We both had to be patient during the difficult years of adjustment. Our many years of genuine love are well worth the prayer, perseverance, forgiveness, and quest for understanding that we experienced during the few years of clashes.

121

No petty grudge or legitimate complaint has value compared to persevering in prayer, believing that God will answer, give you wisdom, and work in the hearts of those around you. Like Sam's wife, you never know what God may do, so never give up praying!

ACTION STEPS

* Approach in-laws with a desire to accept, not change them. If your husband's Aunt Sue and Uncle Merle haven't spoken in thirteen years, let it be. Once you are accepted as "part of the family," and have spent some months praying specifically for them, then approach any occasion to speak wisely and cautiously, or else don't intervene at all. Haven't we all learned this at one time or another? Prayer goes much further than human intervention!
* On the other hand, once you have gained trust and respect from in-laws, there are some things you can say that those in the family simply cannot. A friend of mine boldly spoke up at her husband's family meeting about a relative's addiction. Her boldness was met with gratitude and relief, since none of them had wanted to admit it. The family pledged a change in their behavior right then!
* "In-law problems" that are self-inflicted, such as the young wife who runs to her mother and excludes her husband, can be rectified by simple self-control. We truly are to "cleave" which means to "bond" to our spouses, and make our parents, as precious as they are to us, come second.

QUOTABLE QUOTE:

"Oh, my son's my son till he gets him a wife,
But my daughter's my daughter all her life."
— *Dinah Maria Mulock Craik*[1]
(1826-1887)

MEDITATION:

"Therefore shall a man leave his father and mother, and shall cleave unto his wife . . . ."
— Genesis 2:24

GRANDMA:
A Glorious Crown

I will never forget the day my first grandchild, Lindsay, was born. What a happy time! After all the years of raising my own children with all the struggles, I could now see the fruits of my labors in my grandchildren. It was as though life's cycle was completed. First I was a child, then a married adult, then a mother, and then my children were reproducing tiny composites of genes with some of me in them.

When that first squeaky "Grandma" came from Lindsay's mouth, it was like sweet music. Then there were two more babies, then four and five. Now we have seven grandchildren! When I hear of people who have perhaps twenty grandchildren, or family reunions with as many as five hundred people, I think how fortunate they are. Especially if the original mother and father instilled godly values into their children, who did the same with their children.

Every individual in a family counts. The beauty of family does not have to be blighted even when there has been divorce and remarriage. We can accept stepchildren and love them unconditionally, just as we do those who are born into the family. Everyone needs acceptance, and a child of divorce, death, or abandonment needs more attention than those born into the family naturally. It is easy to favor one above another, particularly those who share our physical characteristics or disposition — characteristics that we secretly admire in ourselves. But we must love them all equally.

I admire greatly those grandparents who, because of circumstances, are raising their grandchildren. I read of a famous athlete who attributed all of his success to his grandmother who raised him. What a struggle, but how rewarding!

The Bible says that an old man's (and woman's) grandchildren are his crowning glory.[1] What a privilege to wear that glorious crown!

ACTION STEPS
* Are you a mother? Remember to look at the big picture the next time you are exasperated

with those children. They will one day give you children that will make your heart burst with pride. What you do with them, they will learn to do with their children. Instill goodness into their characters and godliness into their lives to make a long-range investment.

• What about the victims of broken homes in your family, can you do something to make them feel more welcome?

• Did you miss having a large family to share with? When our family was scattered across the country, Edwin and I learned to invite missionaries, singles and widows into our home for family and holiday celebrations. Become a blessing to others and see how fast your "family" grows!

THOUGHTS TO PONDER:

"Children's children are a crown to the aged, and parents are the pride of their children."

— Proverbs 17:6 NIV

"Even when I am old and gray, do not forsake me, O God, till I declare your power to the next generation . . . . ' "

— Psalm 71:18 NIV

"May you live to see your children's children."

— Psalm 128:6 NIV

FIVE

THE
FIBER
OF
MEN

MEN:
They're Human, Too

M uch is said today about how men treat women, but we rarely hear about how women treat men. We need to admit that as women we are not always in the right in relationship to men. There is a plethora of advice in women's magazines about how to appeal to a man sexually, and how to live with his "male ego." Let's remember that beyond a man's ego and sexuality lies a real human being, a regular "guy." Men know feelings of hurt, embarrassment, failure and tenderness, just as women do.

I overheard a woman recently talking about her husband in a deprecating way while he stood there mute, not knowing what to say. I cringed inside wishing she would stop telling the personal details and embarrassing moments of his life. This was a human being she was talking about! He was obviously respected by others, but his wife took center stage by getting some laughs at his expense.

A woman's tendency to treat a man as if he has no feelings seems to begin in adolescence, when girls run roughshod over boys' feelings, turning them down for dates and telling everyone that they did, or spitefully making fun of the boy who doesn't return some flirting gesture. We know this is a mark of immaturity, but some women simply don't mature beyond that point.

We must accept the differences between women and men, but recognize the similarities as well. We are all human, all with fragile feelings, all sensitive to others' opinions of us to some degree. Let's respect the humanness and human dignity of others, even men! Learn to laugh at yourself and respect others.

ACTION STEPS

It is easy to fall into a habit of deprecation humor. If you are constantly using someone in your family or group of friends to laugh about, think it over. "Oh, it doesn't bother him," is not really a valid statement. If he is alive and breathing, he is affected by the words of others as that is part of being human. When you feel an urge to put down someone you are close to, perhaps a husband, or say something ugly about him, stop yourself and take time to think it through. Often, when we have felt slighted, we lash out at others, sometimes covering our revenge with humor. Check it out! Commit this verse to memory: "Be devoted to one another in brotherly love; give preference to one another in honor."[1]

QUOTABLE QUOTES:
"If ever two were one, then surely we. If ever man were loved by wife, then thee; If ever wife were happy in a man, Compare with me ye women if you can."
> — *Anne Bradstreet[2]*
> *(1612-1672)*

CHANGING HUSBANDS:
The Divine Task

Meshed and blessed, or riven and torn apart — in general, the marriages of my acquaintances over the years have eventually fallen into one category or the other. My friend, Elizabeth, is lively, warm and funny, but I was deeply concerned about the direction she was taking when she told me her marriage was in trouble. She and her husband, Jim, had what divorce lawyers call "irreconcilable differences." Their opinions on everything differed, and she had fallen into the habit of criticizing and finding fault with almost everything he did.

Elizabeth did not realize how much unforgiveness she had toward Jim. She was in bondage to an image of what she thought her husband should be, and could not accept that he was otherwise. She worked arduously to correct her husband's imperfections, "for his sake," she reasoned — but mostly for hers.

Jesus Christ meant it when He said He would make us free.[1] We need the freedom to love, care for, and minister to our families. Nagging, worrying, fault-finding, correcting — these bind both us and our husbands. In the extreme, if the husband doesn't change, the wife changes husbands.

Fortunately, Elizabeth was determined to make her marriage work, and Jim agreed to see the Christian marriage counselor she carefully selected. After just two sessions, Jim canceled because of business demands. Elizabeth, though angry at first, kept going, and a gradual change began to occur. To her surprise, she changed, and as she changed, Jim did, too! Eighteen months later, I visited with Elizabeth and Jim, and they were like two new people — happier and more in love than ever before.

Whenever we focus on any person, for good or bad, we are sure to leave God as a blur in the background. Like Elizabeth, we need Him in our foreground, guiding our steps!

As we fasten our gaze on Him, and leave our men where they belong — in His capable hands — the Holy Spirit will do the work He alone is divinely qualified to do.

ACTION STEPS

* Have you, like Elizabeth perhaps, become focused on the flaws in your husband? Or have you tried to remedy things by human means such as nagging and correcting? Take it to the Lord! If you are unsure of how to pray, perhaps this pattern of prayer will help you get started:

1. Forgive him for everything you haven't forgiven. (At first, this process is lengthy, but after daily practice, you'll be racking your brain for his flaws.)

2. Thank God for all the good qualities in him you can think of.

3. Purge yourself of all selfish motives. Ask God to make him a godly man, just because it will please God.

4. Pray scriptures over him, inserting his name in them, such as the entire chapter of Psalm 112, and this:

   "I keep asking that the God of our Lord Jesus Christ, the glorious Father, may give [your husband's name] *the Spirit of wisdom and revelation, so that* [name] *may know him better. I pray also that the eyes of* [name's] *heart may be enlightened in order that* [name] *may know the hope to which he has called* [name], *the riches of his glorious inheritance in the saints, and his incomparably great power for us who believe."* [2]

5. Thank God in advance for hearing your prayers. Praise Him with a heart full of gratitude, naming everything you can think of to be thankful for.

* Watch your mouth for negative words. If you want to say something negative to your husband, stop and whisper a prayer to see if it measures up to what the Spirit wills.

HE SAID:

"Women who marry men with obvious problems thinking they can change them after marriage, are deceiving their own hearts. 'All he needs is the love of a good woman,' is the classic statement of women who marry alcoholics and then live to regret it. All a man really needs is God. A good woman can help — but a man needs God!"

— Edwin Louis Cole [3]

SHE SAID:

"Your freedom to achieve, to seize opportunities, and to strive to be all that you can be, does not give you the freedom to run over other people, or to move in opposition to authority or to God."

— Nancy Corbett Cole [4]

JUST A THOUGHT:

"Let us let Him clasp our hands a little tighter, and trust Him a little more than ever before — that our paths may be straighter and gladder than in the past."

— Corrie ten Boom[5]

DIFFERENCES:
Fine Print People vs. Headliners

C urrent brain research is proving that men and women are different.[1] Most Bible students know this, but now we are discovering how we differ scientifically. One major difference involves language. A woman's brain generates up to twice as much language as a man's. The result is that although men and women may be on the same "wave length," and reach the same conclusions, women have far more to say about it than men. Women are "fine print people," and men are "headliners."

Working in a predominantly male field, my friend Tammy was frustrated that men in business meetings shifted uncomfortably while she meticulously went over important details. It seemed like the harder she tried to validate her point, the less they agreed. At home, Tammy's husband often stared vacantly at the television while she talked, which infuriated her.

A Christian women's seminar sparked her to try a new strategy. She studiously prepared for her next business meeting. When it was her turn, she stated a recent problem, gave two considerations in dealing with it, then submitted her recommendation. To her astonishment, the men agreed first, then asked for more details. She went back to her office smiling, knowing she had learned to use her God-given talents as a woman, but present them succinctly for men.

That night at dinner, she gave her husband the headlines of her day. After dinner, while they cleaned up the dishes, she supplied all the details, and found she was able to talk as much as she wanted without being interrupted or ignored.

Have you ever recognized the differences between you and your husband . . . boss . . . father . . . son? Often women complain bitterly that a man doesn't think or act more like them. We need to accept differences between sexes, just as we accept differences in other people. And, when we know we can accommodate the other's differences, it doesn't hurt us to try!

ACTION STEPS

* Reflect on your relationships with men. Have you expected others to think or express themselves like you do? Concentrate on becoming a truly empathetic friend, colleague, wife or mother to the men in your life. Recognize their weaknesses, as well as yours. Discipline yourself to give out only what they are able to take in.

* If someone interrupts you to ask what your point is, it is not just rude but probably a pretty accurate signal that you are talking too much! The next time you want to give information to a man — whether it's an idea you want to tell the pastor; a business or sales presentation; a closing argument before a judge; a report on the kids to your husband — get to the point! Put your "bottom line" close to the top and give details sparingly. Don't insist that someone listen to an entire monologue just so you can give your point in your way! Fill in the details at your leisure after the listener has the headlines and you'll both be less frustrated.

NANCY'S THOUGHTS:

I have often wondered why God made women to be "detail" people. These are just thoughts, but does it have to do with women being "the heart of the home" (which is acutely felt in a woman's sudden absence)? Did God give us a unique way of picking up all the details of the home and fitting them together to produce the love and richness of family life that only comes through us?

I think of Mary, Jesus' mother, and how she pondered in her heart the unusual events of Jesus' childhood. The Bible doesn't say Joseph did. It says Mary did. The virtuous woman written of in Proverbs 31 took care of the details of her household that transformed it into a warm, loving home. If this idea is at least partly true, then God is the One Who made us like we are to be the binding, loving force that strengthens our marriage and family.

HE SAID:

"Do not insist on 'your way' or 'no way' at all. Given the ultimatum, a man will choose 'no way' at all."

— Edwin Louis Cole[2]

SHE SAID:

"Go to work on yourself! Change can come in an instant, but usually we have to work on things day by day."

— Nancy Corbett Cole[3]

MEDITATIONS:

"Even a fool is thought wise if he keeps silent, and discerning if he holds his tongue."
— Proverbs 17:28 NIV

"Words from a wise man's mouth are gracious, but a fool is consumed by his own lips. At the beginning his words are folly; at the end they are wicked madness — and the fool multiplies words . . . ."
— Ecclesiastes 10:12-14 NIV

INFATUATION:
Run for Your Life!

Butterflies in the stomach. Sweaty palms. Misspoken words that make you both laugh. The same feelings that make falling in love charming and dreamy can make infatuation deadly and nightmarish. Infatuation with a person who is married to someone else, or by a married individual with a single person, can cause deep wounds and heartbreaks.

Sudden infatuation with a member of the opposite sex can easily arise when you share interests with someone. Even the most upstanding people who do not premeditate romance can fall into it. I met two Christian women who had switched husbands because of infatuation. Each had become enamored of the friend's spouse, divorce followed and new unions were made. But neither felt better off nor were they happy. Each had deep regrets, felt trapped, and were deeply mistrustful of their spouses and friends. I'll never forget one of them lamenting about the other, "She's using my silver and my china, and eating at my table!" Her sincere regret found its voice in the material realm, but the hurt was obviously far deeper.

The old saying goes, "The grass is always greener on the other side." You may think you have found your soul mate in a man, perhaps someone you sing with or work with at church or on the job. You find yourselves thrown together for a purpose which, as you share it, bonds you. Intimate feelings stir and confidences are exchanged. But when the high emotional tide ebbs, the cold wave of reality hits and you wonder, "What have I done?" The "walking on clouds" feeling simply does not last. The bitter, cold reality of heartache, yours and others, is far more horrible to experience than the temporary emptiness of walking away from a dangerous situation.

The wise thing is to "guard your affections."[1] Flee infatuation with the wrong man!

ACTION STEPS

* If you find yourself in a situation where feelings are coming up in you that you know are wrong, run, don't walk from it. Get away in any way possible.
* Confide in someone you trust such as your pastor or counselor (not a gossip!), and let infatuation cool off. If you are working daily with the object of your affections, take a few days off to get alone with God, delve into the Bible and let God give you His perspective. When you go back, avoid personal conversation. Just be your pleasant self without getting too deep.
* There was a very famous book called *Anna Karenina* by the great Russian author, Leo Tolstoy. Anna becomes infatuated and her life ends in tragedy. What a great lesson to reinforce on our minds!

LET'S PRAY:

Father, teach me to guard my heart. Guide me into relationships that are chosen by You and steer me away from becoming infatuated with men who are wrong for me. Instill faithfulness and fidelity in me, Lord, and keep my steps from sliding by Your wonderful keeping power. In Jesus' name I pray. Amen.

WORTH QUOTING:

"Small habits well pursued betimes
May reach the dignity of crimes."
— *Hannah More*[2]
(1745-1833)

SIX

SPINNING THE SITUATION

HOPE:
For Hopeless Situations

Sometimes situations in life demand action that is contrary to our ordinary style of living. Drastic circumstances require drastic actions.

Alice is a friend of mine who lives with impeccable style and grace, complemented equally by her charm and wit. She arouses my admiration and my curiosity for working full time, yet keeping both a sense of humor and a fastidiously clean house.

As she puts it, her husband, John, "was not himself" a few years ago when he suddenly became enamored of another woman and began spending weekends away. Alice suffered personal hurt and rejection. She was humiliated at work and church where she gave excuses for his absences.

During this time, she spent several weekends with me and we prayed often. As we prayed at the beginning of one weekend, she said, "Nancy, I feel led to anoint my furniture and John's car with oil. He left his car at home this weekend. Will you pray in agreement with me?"

I really had no idea what Alice had in mind, and I admit I cringed when I imagined her elegant furniture spotted with oil. When we reached her house, Alice found her olive oil, and as we agreed in prayer together, she tipped the bottle and began freely bathing every piece of furniture with it! The onslaught continued — the damask couch, tailored high back chairs, walnut dining set — until all the furniture was anointed. Alice was gripped with faith. She then marched out to the garage and poured oil on John's gorgeous car.

When we finished praying, we went on to enjoy the weekend, but she never complained or murmured about her situation or her husband. Within weeks John repented and humbly asked for forgiveness which Alice freely gave, as did the church. Alice's furniture was never the worse for the oil, but her faith increased as she tossed aside the natural for the supernatural. She in fact changed the course of her marriage by acting in faith.

Alice still arouses both my admiration and curiosity, but even more than those, I am deeply proud of her uncommon courage in the face of what seemed certain failure. The drastic actions in drastic circumstances made her more of a woman to her friends and husband.

God does not require the same actions from everyone. He may impress upon you something entirely different. Just follow Him!

ACTION STEPS
* When you are facing a crisis, do not feel confined to do what you have always done. Be sensitive to the Holy Spirit to lead you in any direction.
* Remember in the crisis that God is FOR you, not against you; He will lead you when you persevere in prayer.
* Be willing to step out in faith and take drastic action when the Lord leads.
* Anointing a house with oil might be a good idea anytime. A friend did it with her college dorm room and said her roommate noticed their room seemed peaceful from then on.

LET'S PRAY:
Father, I thank You that Jesus Christ is the hope of glory. Because of Jesus, we have hope. Lord, You know the turmoil in my life at this moment. Please infuse me with Your peace to ride out and overcome the turmoil. Increase my hope and faith in Your divine presence in these and all circumstances. In Jesus' name I pray. Amen.

MEDITATIONS:
"And from the days of John the Baptist until now the kingdom of heaven suffereth violence, and the violent take it by force."

— Matthew 11:12

"And Jesus said unto them, Because of your unbelief: for verily I say unto you, If ye have faith as a grain of mustard seed, ye shall say to this mountain, Remove hence to yonder place; and it shall remove; and nothing shall be impossible unto you."

— Matthew 17:20

SWEET POETRY:
"Hope is the thing with feathers —
That perches in the soul —
And sings the tune without the words —
And never stops — at all —"

— *Emily Dickinson*[1]
(1830-1886)

QUOTABLE QUOTES:

"Many Christians want the excitement of a reply from God, but not the pain of the struggle."
— Edith Schaeffer[2]

"It is not in the still calm of life, or in the repose of a pacific station, that great challenges are formed . . . . Great necessities call out great virtues."
— Abigail Adams[3]
(1744-1818)

"Hope is the essential ingredient to make it through life. It is the anchor of the soul."
— Barbara Johnson[4]

BLOWING IT:
Could the Ground Open Up, Please?

Do you ever feel as though you are on a streak of blowing it? You may say the wrong thing, or do something presumptuously that turns out wrong. I have made some serious blunders that seemed to take aeons to straighten out.

I once hurt the feelings of a close friend by plunging into a situation without consulting the Lord. Verbal apologies did not mend her wounds. I could have let it go, saying her unforgiveness was her problem since I admitted my guilt. But friendship is precious, so I persisted and wrote a letter of apology. When I put my apology in writing, she had the time to meditate on it and become forgiving. The incident marked a closer intimacy in our friendship.

When we take our mistakes to God, He lovingly forgives us. The situation may not immediately clear up, but we have given it over to the Lord who can then move on our behalf.

One time Edwin and I had to repent of buying a car presumptuously. Unfortunately, it was still in the driveway when we finished praying, and it was there the next day and the next — and the next. But although we had bought a "lemon" without God's blessing on it, God eventually helped us get rid of it. God healed us and taught us a lesson well!

If you have "blown it" and wish the ground would open and swallow you, *remember we all make mistakes.* We may strive for perfection but invariably we fail in one way or another. Getting up and going on, not letting "end of the world" feelings take hold in our hearts, but accepting God's full forgiveness and acceptance, is a key to successful living.

ACTION STEPS

Blown it? Even if your error would not be considered a "sin," confess it out to God and ask Him to heal you from the embarrassment or feelings of failure.

* Do you have a friend who may need a letter from you like mine did? Believe me, it's worth the stamp!
* Have you ever felt like it was the "end of the world" and still get the feelings of shame when you remember it? It's not too late to clear that up. Go back to the situation in your memory, confess it all out to the Lord, ask Him for wisdom, and begin looking at it through His eyes. As you do, such incidents become smaller and less significant. After all, you have not "blown it" in the most important aspect of life — making Jesus your Lord and Savior.
* Feeling accepted by God is a key to a healthy relationship with Him, as well as with yourself. The best way to fully appreciate and absorb the acceptance God has for you is to meditate, such as: "He has made us accepted in the Beloved."[1] "But God showed his great love for us by sending Christ to die for us while we were still sinners."[2] Also, meditate on God's love.

TRY THIS:

Paint a picture in your mind of Jesus trudging to the Cross, beaten up, His head bleeding. He is dizzy and staggering from the loss of blood and blows to the head. Now see Him on the cross, Roman soldiers handling Him roughly as they nail his hands and feet, Jesus agonizing every time they touch Him. Now see Jesus looking up through the bruises and dried blood, forgiving His persecutors and exclaiming, "It is finished." He means that He has given His life for you, even before you accepted Him as your Savior.

Let that image sink into your heart and mind, for that is truly what Jesus did. Jesus didn't die after we tried to become "perfect Christians." He died while we were in our sin. If you were accepted by Him then, how much more are you now. Hallelujah!

It's enough to make you shout for joy.

QUOTABLE QUOTES:

"Jesus loves me — this I know, For the Bible tells me so."
— *Anna Bartlett Warner*[3]
(1827-1915)

"If we do not see as much as we need or want to see, then we must tell it to the Lord. He will heal our eyes so that we see that the love of God is far greater than anything else."
— *Corrie ten Boom*[4]

DISCRIMINATION:
Follow Esther

Every woman experiences times when it seems being a man would be more convenient — for example, when getting a car repaired, requesting a promotion, negotiating on the telephone, or raising sons without a father. We can be tempted to feel inferior, but I for one am thankful that I'm a woman! Women have strengths that men don't have. For example, we have the strength to handle childbirth!

We need to recognize our womanly strengths. My daughter's boss once instructed her, as a prosecuting attorney, to "act more manly." She tried a masculine approach during her next trial and lost the first case of her career, so she returned to her own unique style.

Discrimination, harrassment and persecution are as old as mankind, and are not limited to sex, but exist with age, ethnicity, economics — all of life. As long as fallen human nature exists, we will find bias, prejudice, manipulation, exploitation and other ills.

The biblical life of Esther, a Hebrew orphan living in exile, teaches women to overcome such plights. Obeying her uncle, Mordecai, young Esther auditioned at the palace and gained the king's favor, becoming a prestigious but powerless queen. Keeping her Hebrew heritage a secret, she soon learned that her race was to be exterminated by the king's order. She promised Mordecai to petition the king, uttering the immortal words, "If I perish, I perish."[1]

What courage!

Esther approached the king, which would cost her her life if he refused her, and was granted his presence at a luncheon. With political savvy that belied her humble beginnings, she invited him again the next day, and there announced that she was a Hebrew and asked for the lives of her people.

The book of Esther makes no mention of God, yet we see Him move powerfully through her to save the entire Jewish race. Likewise, when we act in integrity before God, without manipulating, flirting, or relying on ourselves, God will make a way for us! This is our heritage as women and His pleasure as our Father.

When faced with sex discrimination, intimidation, or situations requiring great strength, we must remember we have the mind of Christ and the power of God to overcome every obstacle. God within us is the victor!

ACTION STEPS

* As Christians, we have what no others have — a powerful God living with and in us Who is concerned about every detail of our lives. The next time you face an intimidating situation, think of how you would feel if a huge, imposing man were hovering around you, ready to demand that you are heard or taken seriously. Then, act like He is there — because you have Jesus Who is that Presence that looks out for your every need!
* If you are raising children alone, remember God is with you as the Father of the fatherless.[2] A successful Christian musician was raised by a single mother who always set an extra place at the table for Jesus. He grew up feeling like Jesus was right there in the house and never went through the rebellious stage that many young men experience. God will give you divinely inspired ideas to take care of His children!
* Stay submitted to those in authority over you. God gives victory to those who are in His Will! The next time you are up for a promotion, negotiating a deal, or promoting a cause, pray using His Word, such as: *"The king's* [decision-maker's] *heart is in the hand of the Lord, he directs it like a watercourse wherever he pleases."*[3]
"He upholds the cause of the oppressed and gives food to the hungry. The Lord sets prisoners free . . . ."[4]
"For promotion cometh neither from the east, nor from the west, nor from the south. But God is the judge: he putteth down one, and setteth up another."[5]
* We can truthfully say that life isn't fair. If you have not yet reached that conclusion, go take a ballet class. Some people just have what it takes, and others don't! But we needn't believe that life is *against* us. That cannot be. Jesus is the "way, the truth, and the life."[6] He provided the way to heaven, His Word is our ultimate truth, and He gives us life more abundantly[7] than we could have in any other way. In fact, Jesus is our life. With Him living through us, we cannot fail.

MEDITATIONS:
". . . If God be for us, who can be against us?"
— Romans 8:31

"Blessed is the man . . . [whose] delight is in the law of the Lord; and in his law doth he meditate day and night . . . whatsoever he doeth shall prosper."
— Psalm 1:1-3

TRAPPED:
Finding the Way Out

"Is there no way out?" Many women get trapped in circumstances and cannot find a way out, but there IS a way!

I asked this of the Lord when I felt trapped in a minuscule, noisy, seven-hundred square-foot parsonage. The bungalow was attached to the second church we pastored, subjecting us to constant surveillance by the congregation. Our three small children filled one tiny bedroom by night and crowded a small living area by day. As we faithfully endured year after year, the children grew, the cramping increased, and I became more overwhelmed and distressed.

The noise alone was unsettling. Outside our tiny front yard, dirt trucks going to and from a large construction site kept the street in a constant filthy uproar. Directly overhead, planes roared from the bustling airport nearby. Our bedroom faced the busy street where the noise of trucks at night was overpowered only by shrieks of trains on the railroad tracks a block away.

After pouring out my heart to God one day, I began to read my Bible. Suddenly a verse from Psalm 91 leaped out like a living entity: "Surely I shall deliver thee . . . from the noisome pestilence." Wow! As I excitedly turned pages, Psalm 118:5 sprang to life: "I called upon the Lord in distress: the Lord answered me and set me in a large place." God was speaking directly to me through His Word, and I found myself crying in joy and praise.

A short time later, God planted us in a larger church in a beautiful city where He gave me a spacious house with quiet, park-like surroundings. Hallelujah! I realize now that parsonage was a learning experience, like a three-year training school. "In God's time," we often say, but this was a real lesson of what that means. There were many lessons to come, but I learned not to worry about circumstances — the Lord knows them all and He will deliver!

ACTION STEPS

- If you cannot in any way control your circumstances, accept them and turn them over to the Lord, perhaps like this:
  1. Admit that unless God intervenes, there is no way out.
  2. Ask God to intervene.
  3. Use favorite scriptures or Bible illustrations. For example, say out loud to God, "I know You made a way for Israel to escape from Egypt, and I know You will make a way for me!"
  4. Commit yourself to accept the solution God brings. Remember Naaman who had incurable leprosy, but did not want to do what the prophet told him. When he resigned himself to follow directions and dip in the muddy river, he was instantly healed![1]
  5. Praise God for the solution.

"YOU CAN QUOTE ME!"

"I thank God that I am endued with such qualities that if I were turned out in the Realm in my petticoat, I were able to live in any place in Christendom."
— *Queen Elizabeth I*[2]
(1533-1603)

"The more perfect our patience, the more completely we possess our souls."
— *Susan Muto*[3]

"God knows and is interested both in the hardest problems we face and the tiniest details that concern us. He knows how to put everything in place, like a jigsaw puzzle, to make a beautiful picture."
— *Corrie ten Boom*[4]

FEAR:
The Big Bear

One summer when our children were small, we went camping in Yosemite National Park. A friend who worked for an outdoor equipment company loaned us top-of-the-line camping equipment so even I, a novice camper, was comfortable.

At night, to keep from attracting bears, we followed the ranger's instructions, including leaving the ice chest we had for milk outside our tent. One night some noises startled me out of my sleep. I lay still inside my sleeping bag, listening intently. The noises were coming from where we left the ice chest. Then I heard sounds like something was opening it and a gurgle sound like drinking. It was a BEAR!

I have never been so scared, before or since. I was frozen to my cot, my forehead perspiring and heart pounding. After a short time, which seemed like an eternity, the sounds ceased and I dozed fitfully until morning. As dawn turned to day, I heard Edwin starting the campfire and I rose to start breakfast.

"Edwin," I said, "Did you hear the bear?"

"No," he replied.

I was rather groggy but noticed that the milk carton was intact in the ice chest. I looked for bear tracks and questioned Edwin again about the sounds in the night.

"If there was a bear," he said, "you'd think I would have seen or heard him. I was up in the night with a sore throat, so I drank some milk then walked around until I was sleepy again." Would you believe it, my husband was my bear!

This incident gave me great empathy for people who are fearful. With God as our Father, we really have no reason to be gripped by fear as I was that night. The Bible tells us that perfect love casts out fear because fear has torment.[1] I know that torment! If you are fearful AT ALL, I urge you to open yourself to God for deliverance through His love.

ACTION STEPS

What you can do to be delivered from fear:

1. *Develop a strong sense of God's love.* Say, "He loves me and me especially." Second Timothy 1:7 (NKJV) says, "God has not given us a spirit of fear, but of power and of love and of a sound mind." Love delivers us from fear, leaving us with a sound mind. The more aware we are of God's love, the more aware we are of Him as our protector and guide, who leads us not into dangerous places or situations, but away from them. Quote scriptures of His love daily until it indelibly impresses your mind and heart.

2. *Invest time to know God.* If we are fearful, then we haven't allowed God to permeate us, soul and spirit, with His presence. We don't think He is big enough to take care of us or our family the way we would like. This is from not communing with Him through His Word and in prayer.

3. *Rid yourself of guilt.* The promises of God are for obedient, not disobedient children. When we are disobedient, the inner voice of the Holy Spirit tells us. Once we repent, we don't let ourselves wallow in the guilt of the past but continuually accept Christ's work on the Cross and the complete forgiveness God gives.

4. *Learn to trust God completely.* Once we let our lack of trust in God take over, fear takes hold. We can become fearful not of just one situation, but for our children's safety, our husband's safety, and everyone else that our fear grabs hold of. Some women become so obsessed with fear that they constrain their children. By trusting God with our loved ones, we can work out the balance between being wisely cautious and overprotective.

   Some women also try to control things — their husband, Sunday School class, others' lives — because of fear that if they don't intervene, God won't take care of things. If you are one of these, you have probably had people tell you to stop, yet never understood what you did wrong in the first place. Trust in God and your heart and behavior will fall into place. Psalm 125:1 (NKJV) says: "Those who trust in the Lord are like Mount Zion, which cannot be moved, but abides forever."

5. *Resist the enemy.* Satan will try to keep you in fear, to cripple you from walking by faith. The Bible says: "Do not give the devil a foothold"[2] and "Submit yourselves therefore to God. Resist the devil, and he will flee from you."[3]

MEDITATIONS:

"There is no fear in love; but perfect love casteth out fear: because fear hath torment. He that feareth is not made perfect in love."

— 1 John 4:18

"Behold, God is my salvation; I will trust, and not be afraid: for the Lord Jehovah is my strength and my song; he also is become my salvation."

— Isaiah 12:2

"I sought the Lord, and he answered me; he delivered me from all my fears."

— Psalm 34:4 NIV

DEATH AND GRIEF:
You Don't Stop Loving

G rief is a healthy, normal process unless it does not run its course. The death of a loved one is traumatic, no matter the age of survivor or deceased. My mother died in the prime of life, unexpectedly collapsing in the hallway one night after dinner. Her absence left a vacancy in my heart that nothing seemed to fill.

Though we lived on opposite coasts, Mother and I visited as often as possible. She accepted me as I was, never criticizing my husband, our child-rearing, occupations — nothing. Her letters were sources of inspiration, advice and counsel. Our phone calls were spiced with laughter such as the night I called and interrupted her as she cooked lobsters. One got away and she thought it was racing toward her. How we laughed when she shrieked, "It's after me!"

I mourned so deeply when she died that it affected my relationship with the Lord. I asked Him, "Why?" until the question became an accusation. One night I threw myself on the floor and cried, "Lord, look how I'm suffering! Help me!" I don't know if my eyes were open or closed, but immediately a bright light flooded my vision. In the light was a cross, and I had the impression of a voice saying, "Look how *I* suffered." I felt like a speck in the universe when I saw Jesus, God's Son, dying for me. I repented sincerely.

Love does not stop at death. I still love and miss my mother. But today I rejoice in a Heavenly Father Who loved me even through the death of His Son — a Father Who will never grow old, take ill, or die.

ACTION STEPS
* Make it a goal this year to contact everyone you love by letter or phone call. Make sure they know you love them, even if your relationship has been strained before. Don't

talk long enough for differences or old problems to come up; just leave a positive impression, and let it go at that.

• When friends, colleagues, or fellow church members experience a death in the family, you do not need to shy away from them. You also don't need to try to console them. Just take something, a hot dish or dessert, flowers or just a card, expressing your sympathy. Your actions speak louder, and probably are more consoling, than your words.

QUOTABLE QUOTES:
"When I am dead, my dearest,
Sing no sad songs for me;
Plant thou no roses at my head,
Nor shady cypress tree.
Be the green grass above me
With showers and dewdrops wet;
And if thou wilt, remember
And if thou wilt, forget."

> — *Christina Georgina Rossetti*[1]
> *(1830-1894)*

"Then, at that moment, when all the world seemed to be crumbling and slipping from beneath my feet, the Comforter, the blessed Holy Spirit, whom Jesus had sent, rose up within me and revealed Jesus in such a precious way, made the will of God so sweet, showed the prepared mansions so real that I shouted 'Glory' by the death bed of Robert Semple, from whom I had never dreamed of parting."

> — *Aimee Semple McPherson*[2]

SEVEN

PHYSICAL THREADS

APPEARANCE:
Confidence Conveyed

Most women rush in the morning to get ready for work, to see a husband off, or to send children to school. Grooming is just a way of life. Their hair is passable, their clothes are neat, and the children nearly always look nice — at least when they send the children out.

But what about *your* appearance? Do you try to "just get by," saying perhaps, "It doesn't matter how I look — no one sees me"?

A friend of mine said this to herself one morning as she rushed to her government job. "After all," she reasoned, "my dress is decent, and that's better than a lot of other women in my office!"

That day the state governor paid an unannounced visit to her building. Always equal to any challenge, she squared her shoulders, smoothed her dress and marched out of her office to join the other workers who were greeting him. She lived through the moment, but the next week the pictures of the governor's visit were posted and there she was — immortalized on film as a dowdy frump!

Every day someone important sees you — YOU! Be honest — aren't you more relaxed and confident when you are well-groomed? Generally, those who are sloppily dressed have sloppy houses, too. Isn't life more peaceful when children pick up after themselves, when we enforce rules, and when we discipline ourselves in the same way to have a neat, attractive appearance?

Your relationship with others improves when your appearance improves.

And, appearance is important in conveying an image of Christlikeness to the world around us. We don't have to get all dressed up to go to the grocery store, but we can be tasteful, neat, modest and always clean.[1]

ACTION STEPS
* Make a mental checklist of things you can improve, and concentrate on improving one

157

each week. One week hair, one week doing your ironing in advance, one week learning a new makeup technique.

◆ Almost every closet needs help. A friend of mine used to go through and give away everything she had not worn for two or three years. If she was not using it, she thought she may as well give it to someone who will. You might need to get rid of everything that is unbecoming, and gradually start putting things together to make up new outfits.

◆ Think back to your early teens when you didn't want to wear the same thing or do your hair in the same way in a two-week period. Concentrate on regaining some of that zest for personal appearance!

BEAUTY TIPS:

When time or finances permit, why not try these "beautifiers"?

— Reserve a block of time for yourself once a week to pamper yourself: take a leisurely bubble bath, then give yourself a manicure. Put on some lovely, soothing, music, and just remind yourself that, since you are created in God's image, you are beautiful!

— Have a professional color analysis done to discover which colors are best for your skin tones and hair.

— Contact a local department store and find out if their cosmetics department books appointments for complimentary makeovers to give you a chance to learn new makeup application techniques to try at home later.

QUOTABLE QUOTES:

"A little of what you call frippery [finery] is very necessary towards looking like the rest of the world."

> — *Abigail Adams (1744-1818)*[2]

"Adornment is never anything except a reflection of the heart."
> — *Remark by Coco Chanel*[3]
> *(1883-1970)*

"A place for everything and everything in its place."
> — *Isabella Mary Beeton*[4]
> *(1836-1865)*

"We need to be concerned more with how our lives reflect His love, His holiness, His obedience, than with the latest witnessing techniques."
> — *Rebecca Manley Pippert*[5]

EXERCISE:
Revitalize Your Well-Being

When I was just over thirty years old, I played in a softball game at a church picnic. I got three good hits and ran the bases all three times as fast as I could. When it was over I was tired, but I didn't know the half of it until the next morning. My legs hurt so badly that I could barely swing them out of the bed. I must have been a sight discreetly picking up my legs with my hands to get into the car! I could hardly believe I was that out of shape. My life-long exercise program began that weekend.

Exercise is important physically, emotionally, mentally, and in our ability to handle stress. Exercise revitalizes us as it pumps oxygen into our brains, joints and muscles. Most people today are aware of the benefits of fitness. It is great to "plug in" to that awareness with something you like. For me, it's tennis and walking. When I play tennis regularly, I am so full of energy that I often jump in the pool for a swim after a match. I also love walking. I love to pray as I walk a few miles around my neighborhood at twilight.

Of course, these activities are easier when you don't have children at home or work 8-to-5. Running a household, plus possibly a job, and shuffling kids around certainly gives our bodies a workout of sorts, but not the kind of invigorating exercise that relaxes and refreshes us. Where there isn't time to exercise, we have to make time. For many years I sat at a desk in an office, so I tried to go out for exercise every lunch hour. In the evening when the chores were done, I would also follow an exercise book to keep my body flexible. I remember a period when I quit flexibility exercises only to be horrified later when I reached down to touch my toes and stopped about four inches from the floor, unable to go further.

Stiffness and tension show up not just in our bodies, but in our relationships. When we are uncomfortable, we become irritable and grumpy with others. When we exercise, we have a greater sense of well-being which promotes a healthy mind and spirit, and relationships with others.

ACTION STEPS

* Cardiovascular health is as important as muscle strength and flexibility. Aerobic exercise, such as walking, jogging and biking, is the best way to promote cardiovascular health. Walking is one of the fastest-growing sports today. Your local YMCA or community recreation department may have aerobic exercise or walking programs.
* The simplest and cheapest way for many of us to get a total body work-out today is through videos. If you have a VCR and do not want to join a gym, there are wonderful videos (like Kathy Smith's) that take you from basics through vigorous body toning and aerobic workouts. If you are older and do not want that strenuous pace, Angela Lansbury has a good video that puts us through some not so energetic steps, but still helps tone our bodies and keep them supple and strong.
* Often we compare ourselves to beautiful bodies in magazines or at a gym, and give up on fitness before we even try. Or we think we have to exercise at a level of intensity we feel we can't attain, or for a length of time that is impossible in our schedule. Or we think we're just too old to start. Well, current studies show that the intensity and duration of the exercise do not matter, but that REGULARITY is the key to muscle tone and cardiovascular health. And it really doesn't take that much exercise to begin to have one of the beautiful bodies you see in pictures. Although some people do have better ''genes'' for a shapely body than others, you can at least have the pleasure of knowing your body is physically fit.
Regarding age, other studies show that the same amount of exercise, begun at any age, will give the same results as if you had started when you were young. In fact, if you are older and really ambitious, you could check into some organized athletics. They make it easier for older people to win by placing them in categories without younger people. Do some biking, swimming and running, then try a triathlon, or start the tennis program in your community. Doing something fun will help you stick with it.

GRACEFUL GROWTH:
Youth to Maturity

We grow old either gracefully or grouchily. I love to be around women who accept the age they are and continue growing in their minds and spirits. Being a little older myself, I realize this gracefulness is something they started working on when they were young. Some women work on being positive. Others take every setback, which we all have, as a heavy blow. Whatever is in the heart eventually reveals itself on the face with expressions that solidify over the years.

An older woman once loaned money to a church purely as an investment, and was particularly cantankerous about receiving her interest payments on time. When Edwin began to pastor there, he took a wise and gracious church official along to visit this woman to see if they could become friendly with her. The visit was very difficult, for she would not receive their warmth or friendship. As they left her, the older man remarked, "When people get as old as she is, the charm and personality wear off and all that is left is character."

How true, that what I am building into my character today will become "me" when I am old. How important it is to build the fruits of the Holy Spirit into my life: love, joy, peace, longsuffering, gentleness, goodness, faith, meekness and temperance.[1]

A woman prison minister wrote to me recently. She said, "My prison ministry of 14 years is going well and God is blessing the efforts. I love Him so." She signed off with her name and this, "66 and still growing — With all the immutable riches of Christ still ahead, why not?"

Which do you want to be like, the woman who begrudges her old age, who has not built a Christlike character into her life, or the other who is still happily engaged in bringing cheer and God's Word of hope and salvation to others?

161

ACTION STEPS

* Look at your face in a mirror. Do you see a relaxed, cheerful woman? Remember, if you don't have pleasant expressions on your face now, you won't be able to fake them later without appearing phony. Change your face by purifying your mind of all negative thoughts, "washing" it with the "water by the word,"[2] renewing it daily[3] by reading God's Word and praying. Look at your face after a good time of prayer, and begin to "put on" that kind of a face every day by working from the inside out.

* Start a new prayer list, just for you. Write down the things that most concern you right now and cast those cares[4] on the Lord each morning. Then, with all those burdens now on God's shoulders, begin thinking about "whatsoever things are pure," and "of good report."[5]

* Monitor your thought life. Whenever a negative thought comes across your mind, tell yourself you will not be overcome by the negative. Take "every thought captive"[6] and turn your focus onto the Lord. At night, just before you retire, look at the progress you have made in thinking the way God thinks, and be happy about the grace of the Lord that is changing you.

* Memorize the passage of scripture about the fruits of the Spirit in Galatians 5:22,23.

LET'S PRAY:

Father, I thank You for all the seasons of life. As I grow older, help me to embrace this season as one of joy. Help me to experience each new day joyfully, to do all things with all of my might. Help me to share myself with others and to share my faith in Christ with those I encounter. In Jesus' name I pray. Amen.

LINES THAT WILL LINGER:

"Does the road wind uphill all the way?
Yes, to the very end.
Will the day's journey take the whole long day?
From morn to night, my friend."

> — *Christina Georgina Rossetti*[7]
> *(1830-1894)*

GRACEFUL GROWTH:
Becoming "More Mature"

Do you know an older person who spreads sunshine wherever she goes? Or one who seems to have a cloud hovering over her?

Growing old gracefully is an art you can begin to master now. This is the secret: Accept the limitations of the stage in life where you are. Younger minds are limited without a wide range of experiences to draw from. Older bodies are limited because they cannot do handsprings, maintain high energy or hit the ball like before. Some of us can't even see the ball!

We must accept where we are and realize God uses our abilities and talents at the level of performance we can accomplish. This brings great peace of mind that spills over into an easy smile and sincere concern for others.

Alma is a dear widow of a famous minister. When he died, she discovered that his trusted advisor had misused their entire estate and nothing was left. She was completely destitute and alone. Gone were the accolades of thousands where she graced the platform as her husband spoke. Behind her were the social occasions where she was the guest of honor. Only memories were left of the glorious prayer meetings with great men and women of God. The average person would be embittered — but not Alma! God has miraculously taken care of her through friends and family. She has a song in her heart to praise Him. She writes short notes to me and Edwin regularly, with a Scripture and encouragement that always blesses us.

Her last note started, " 'Are not five sparrows sold for two pennies? Yet not one of them is forgotten by God.'[1] What a reason to sing!" What an inspiration!

You can choose to be like Alma — alive and vibrant at every stage of life. It's the best choice and the best life!

ACTION STEPS

* Have you envied young, energetic people who keep going day and night, or the young beauty who turns heads at stoplights? Repent of your envy. Thank God for the beauty He has placed within you; the wisdom He has given you; the lessons you have learned that you never have to repeat. No matter how young or old you are, you have so many reasons to praise God. Think of the wonderful things that you have in the season of life you are in right now. Meditate on passages from the Word like the one Alma quoted. Begin to rejoice over them every day!

* Ecclesiastes 3:11 (TLB) says: "Everything is appropriate in its own time. But though God has planted eternity in the hearts of men, even so, man cannot see the whole scope of God's work from beginning to end."

* Adopt a spirit of giving like Alma — whether money, goods, or just generous blessings to others that come from the heart of God.

SHE SAID:

"Whatever we find in our hand to do, we are to do it with all our might! This is not a scripture for the young. It is applicable to all our lives, young and old. Every scripture in the Bible is for you. You never outgrow it."

— Nancy Corbett Cole[2]

HE SAID:

"Each day, each month, each year for each person holds an attraction and glory all its own — if we just take the time and make the effort to behold and enjoy it."

— Edwin Louis Cole[3]

THINK ABOUT THIS:

"Stay in Him! Live His plan for you with all your might! Be happy in Him, be happy in your life in Him; be happy in all He gives you and in all He takes away; be happy in what you do; be happy in what you can't do; be happy in all He makes you to be; be happy in what He never allows you to be."

— Anne Ortlund[4]

WORTH QUOTING:

"That it will never come again
Is what makes life so sweet."

— *Emily Dickinson*[5]
(1830-1886)

"Life was meant to be lived, and curiosity must be kept alive. One must never, for whatever reason, turn his back on life."

— *Anna Eleanor Roosevelt*[6]
(1884-1962)

A
FINAL
WORD

A FINAL WORD

Thank you for sharing your time with me in the pages of this book. I hope these stories and truths have uplifted and inspired you. I trust you now realize that you are not alone: Jesus is with you to help you in beautifying and making your own tapestry of life.

When the reality that Christ died for me penetrated my heart years ago, I was standing at my ironing board. I set down my iron, raised my eyes toward heaven and simply said, "Lord, I believe." In that brief moment, I passed from death to life.

The scripture says, "If any man be in Christ, he is a new creature: old things are passed away; behold, all things are become new."[1]

Salvation is both instant and constant. We are instantly saved at the moment we believe, and continually saved as we let go of the old life, and live in the new.

If you have never accepted Jesus Christ into your life in a personal relationship, it doesn't matter where you are or what you are doing, just take a moment and pray this prayer with me now:

"Jesus, I believe that You are my Savior. I believe that You died and rose again and are sitting at the right hand of God to intercede for me. I ask for Your forgiveness for all my sins. I ask Your Holy Spirit to come into my heart right now. I believe Your Word which says, 'If we confess our sins, he is faithful and just to forgive us our sins, and to cleanse us from all unrighteousness.'[2] Thank You for cleansing me, for changing me, and for welcoming me into Your family. I now call You 'Lord,' for I give my life to You, and ask for Your guidance in all that I do. Thank You for hearing and answering me today. Amen."

You have now passed from death to life! It is important that you find a good church, perhaps through the person who led you to this book, and begin your Christian education. Old things are passed away, and today is a brand new day.

ENDNOTES

Foreword
1 Titus 2:4

One — Strands of the Soul

Wisdom: Hope For Us All
1 Proverbs 8:1 NKJV
2 Proverbs 17:28
3 Matthew 21:21,22; 1 John 5:14
4 *God's Covenant for Your Family* (Tulsa: Harrison House, 1982).
5 *Meditations Divine and Moral* (1664). *The Complete Works of Anne Bradstreet*, edited by Joseph R. McElrath and Allan P. Robb, (Boston: Twayne Publishers, 1981).

Understanding: Now I Get It!
1 Proverbs 4:7
2 Luke 6:38
3 "The Poor" from *Familiar Quotations* by John Bartlett (Boston: Little, Brown and Company, 1980).

Forgotten: God Never Forgets
1 Ecclesiastes 11:4 TLB

Imaginations: Willy-Nilly Feelings
1 2 Corinthians 10:5
2 1 John 4:18
3 "Imagination," words by Johnny Burke, music by Jimmy Van Heusen, copyright © 1940 by Bourne Company.

Faith: Or Was That Fantasy?
1 2 Corinthians 10:5
2 Psalm 1:2

Bitterness: From Gloom to Glow
1 *Edith Cavell* by Rowland Ryder (New York: Stein and Day, 1975), October 12, 1915.

Attitudes: Will and Determination
1 Philippians 4:11 NAS
2 1 Timothy 6:6
3 *The Almanac of the Christian World* (Wheaton, IL: Tyndale House Publishers, Inc., 1991-92 edition).
4 *Anne Frank: The Diary of a Young Girl* (New York: Doubleday, 1967).
5 *Masterpieces of Religious Verse*, edited by James Dalton Morrison, "Winds of Fate" (New York: Harper & Row, Publishers, 1948).

6 *The Ballad Book*, edited by MacEdward Leach, "Molly Bawn," 1878 (New York: Harper and Brothers, 1955).

Faithfulness: Count On Me
1 Proverbs 20:6
2 Psalm 31:23 NIV
3 *A Practical Guide to Spiritual Reading* (Denville, NJ: Dimension Books, 1976).
4 *Out of the Saltshaker and Into the World* (Downers Grove, IL: InterVarsity Press, 1979).
5 *Disciplines of the Heart* (Dallas, TX: Word Books, 1987).

Anger: Emotion or Sin?
1 2 Peter 3:18
2 Galatians 5:22
3 Ecclesiastes 7:9

Self-Image: God's Image of Us
1 Psalm 139:17,18 TLB
2 Romans 8:16,17
3 *The Unique Woman* (Tulsa: Honor Books, 1989).
4 *The Unique Woman*.
5 *This Is My Story* (New York: Harper and Brothers, 1937).
6 *Gift from the Sea* (New York: Vintage Books, a division of Random House, 1955).
7 *Steps Along the Way* (Denville, NJ: Dimension Books, 1975).
8 *Disciplines of the Heart* (Dallas, TX: Word Books, 1987).
9 *Disciplines of the Heart*.

Two — Living A Finely Textured Life

Hospitality: Forget the Imperfections
1 Ecclesiastes 11:4 TLB
2 1 Timothy 3:2 TLB
3 *Favorite Poems of Emily Dickinson* (New York: Avenel Books, 1978).
4 *Chanel*, by Edmonde Charles-Roux (New York: Alfred A. Knopf, 1975).

Smile: All The Medicine You Need
1 Proverbs 17:22
2 *Anatomy of an Illness* by Norman Cousins (New York: W. W. Nortonand Company, 1979).
3 "Accentuate the Positive," words by Johnny Mercer, music by Harold Arlen (Harwin Music Corporation, 1944).
4 *With My Whole Heart* (Portland, OR: Multnomah Press, 1987).

Graciousness: The Art of Living
[1] *The Unique Woman* (Tulsa: Honor Books, 1989).
[2] *The Unique Woman.*
[3] *L'abri* (Wheaton, IL: Tyndale House Publishers, 1969).

Single: "One" By One
[1] Proverbs 3:6 NKJV
[2] 2 Corinthians 3:18
[3] Romans 8:28
[4] *The Unique Woman* (Tulsa: Honor Books, 1989).
[5] *The Unique Woman.*
[6] *The Country of the Pointed Firs* (Cambridge, Mass.: Houghton Mifflin Co., The Riverside Press, 1896).

Talents: Too Much to Cram Into Thirty Years
[1] Ecclesiastes 3:1 TLB
[2] *An English Woman's Work Amongst Working Men* (New Britain, Conn.: John A. Williams Publisher).

Addictions: Overcome By Prayer
[1] Sandra Simpson LaSourd, *The Compulsive Woman* (Old Tappan, NJ: Chosen Books, 1987).
[2] *The Unique Woman* (Tulsa: Honor Books, 1989).
[3] *The Unique Woman.*
[4] *Five Girls Who Dared,* collected by Helen Ferris, "Courage Is the Price" (New York: The Macmillan Co., 1931).
[5] *Final Harvest* (Boston: Little, Brown and Company, 1961).

Time: Controlling The Clock
[1] *L'abri* (Wheaton, IL: Tyndale House Publishers, 1969).
[2] *Favorite Poems of Emily Dickinson* (New York: Avenel Books, 1978).
[3] *The Lost Lover,* Act IV., sc.1, printed for R. Bentley in Covent-Garden, London, 1696.

Family Traditions: Making Meaningful Memories
[1] *The Almanac of the Christian World.*
[2] *"America The Beautiful,"* by Katharine Lee Bates (1896).
[3] *Masterpieces of Religious Verse,* "The Landing of the Pilgrim Fathers," st. 10.

Three — Heart Strings

Forgiveness: The Fresh Start
[1] John 20:23 NKJV
[2] Luke 23:34
[3] 1 John 1:9
[4] Revelation 2:4,5 NAS
[5] *Tramp for the Lord* by Corrie ten Boom with Jamie Buckingham (New York: Jove Books, Fleming H. Revell Company, 1972).
[6] *The Unique Woman* (Tulsa: Honor Books, 1989).
[7] *The Unique Woman.*
[8] *The Poetical Works* by C. G. Rossetti (New York: George Olms Verlag Hildesheim, 1970), "Remember" (1862).

Faith and Finance: $7.00 and a Fruitcake
[1] Matthew 28:20 NKJV
[2] *Communication, Sex and Money* (Tulsa: Honor Books, 1987).
[3] Harriet Tubman to her biographer, Sarah H. Bradford (1868).
[4] *The Brownings: Letters and Poetry* by Christopher Ricks, "Aurora Leigh" (1857), (Garden City, NY: Doubleday, 1970).

Waiting: God's Unexpected Answers
[1] Ecclesiastes 11:6
[2] *Stick A Geranium in Your Hat and Be Happy* (Dallas, TX: Word Books, 1990).

Praise: The Reflection of Love
[1] Psalm 33:1 NAS
[2] "Vesalius in Zante" from *Familiar Quotations* by John Bartlett.
[3] *This is That* (Los Angeles: Echo Park Evangelistic Association, Inc., 1923).

Spirit: Feeling the "Nudge"
[1] John 10:27
[2] James 2:20
[3] *The Unique Woman* (Tulsa: Honor Books, 1989).
[4] *The Unique Woman.*
[5] *A Woman's Choice — Living Through Your Problems* (Grand Rapids, MI: Zondervan, 1962).

Submission: The Road to Victory
[1] James 4:7
[2] 2 Corinthians 12:10
[3] John 21:22
[4] "Submission," music by Austin Miles; lyrics by Mrs. R. R. Forman (Winona Lakes, IN: Norman Clayton Publishing Co., a Division of Rodeheaver, Hall-Mack Co., 1934).
[5] *The Unique Woman* (Tulsa: Honor Books, 1989).
[6] *The Unique Woman.*

Prayer: Take Up A Sword!
[1] Judges 4:4-8
[2] Matthew 11:12
[3] *The Unique Woman* (Tulsa: Honor Books, 1989).
[4] *The Unique Woman.*
[5] "Nine Keys to Effective Intercession" (Dallas, TX: Edwin Louis Cole Ministries, © 1992 by Edwin Louis Cole).
[6] *Marrow of Ecclesiastical History* (London: William Du Gard, 1650.)
[7] "The Battle Hymn of the Republic," by Julia Ward Howe (1862).
[8] *Disciplines of the Heart* (Dallas, TX: Word Books, 1987).

Four — Weaving Relationships

Friends: Recognize True Friendship
[1] Proverbs 18:24
[2] *How To Win Friends and Influence People* (New York: Simon and Schuster/Pocket Books, 1981).

[3] *The Poetical Works* (1970), last lines of "Goblin Market" (1862).

Good Times: You Don't Have to Feel Neglected
[1] *The Family Album of Favorite Poems,* edited by P. Edward Ernest (New York: Grossett and Dunlap, 1959) "Solitude," st. 1.
[2] *52 Simple Ways to Tell Your Child "I Love You"* (Nashville, TN: Thomas Nelson Publishers/Oliver-Nelson, 1991).

Childlessness: God's Plans and Ours
[1] 1 Samuel 1:6-20
[2] 1 Samuel 2:21

Moms: Making Moments Count
[1] *The Almanac of the Christian World.*
[2] *The Almanac of the Christian World.*
[3] *Anne Frank: The Diary of a Young Girl* (1952).
[4] "My Mother," from *Original Poems for Infant Minds* (1804).
[5] *Gone With The Wind* (New York: Macmillan, 1936).
[6] *Gift From the Sea* (1955).

Children: Raise Them for the Lord
[1] *Her Son's Wife* (New York: Harcourt, Brace & Co., 1926), chapter 37.
[2] *The Queen Mother* by Elizabeth Longford (New York: William Morrow & Co., 1981).

Christian Education: Proper Dress for War
[1] Proverbs 22:6
[2] Ephesians 6:10-18
[3] Ephesians 6:13-18
[4] Letter to her son, John Quincy Adams; May 8, 1780; from *Familiar Quotations* by John Bartlett.
[5] *A Backward Glance.*
[6] *L'abri* (Wheaton, IL: Tyndale House Publishers, 1969).
[7] *L'abri.*

Delegate: Improve Your Life
[1] *The Home Book of Verse,* edited by Burton Egbert Stevenson (New York: Henry Holt & Co., 1953), "Beauty and Duty."

I Love You: Words of Life
[1] Luke 23:34
[2] *Sonnets of the Portuguese* (Garden City, NY: Doubleday, 1954).
[3] *NIV Women's Devotional Bible* (Grand Rapids, MI: Zondervan Corporation, 1990).
[4] Quoted by *Elizabeth the First, Queen of England,* Neville Williams (New York: E. P. Dutton & Co., 1968), "The Golden Speech" (1601).

Pastor's Wife: Gracious Help
[1] *Gift from the Sea* (1955).

In-Laws: Rewards of Perseverance
[1] *The Home Book of Verse,* "Young and Old."

Grandma: A Glorious Crown
[1] Proverbs 17:6

Five — The Fiber of Men

Men: They're Human, Too!
[1] Romans 12:10 NAS
[2] *American Poetry and Prose,* edited by Norman Foerster, Norman S. Grabo, Russel B. Nye, E. Fred Carlisle and Robert Falk (Cambridge, Mass: Houghton Mifflin Co., 1970), "To My Dear and Loving Husband," (1678).

Changing Husbands: The Divine Task
[1] John 8:36
[2] Ephesians 1:17-19 NIV
[3] *The Unique Woman* (Tulsa: Honor Books, 1989).
[4] *The Unique Woman.*
[5] *Jesus Is Victor* (Old Tappan, NJ: Fleming H. Revell Company/Chosen Books, 1985).

Differences: Fine Print People vs. Headliners
[1] "Sizing Up The Sexes," by Christine Gorman; Time Magazine, © Copyright January 20, 1992.
[2] *The Unique Woman* (Tulsa: Honor Books, 1989).
[3] *The Unique Woman.*

Infatuation: Run For Your Life!
[1] Proverbs 4:23 TLB
[2] "Florio and His Friend" from *Familiar Quotations* by John Bartlett.

Six — Spinning the Situation

Hope: For Hopeless Situations
[1] *Final Harvest* (Boston: Little, Brown and Company, 1961).
[2] *L'abri* (Wheaton, IL: Tyndale House Publishers, 1969).
[3] Letter to her husband, John Adams, January 19, 1780; from *Familiar Quotations* by John Bartlett.
[4] *Stick A Geranium in Your Hat and Be Happy* (Dallas, TX: Word Books, 1990).

Blowing It: Could The Ground Open Up, Please?
[1] Ephesians 1:6 NKJV
[2] Romans 5:8 TLB
[3] *American Hymns Old and New,* edited by Albert Christ-Janer, Charles W. Hughes and Carleton Sprague Smith, "Jesus Loves Me"(1858), (New York: Columbia University Press, 1980).
[4] *Jesus Is Victor* (Old Tappan, NJ: Fleming H. Revell Company/Chosen Books, 1985).

Discrimination: Follow Esther
[1] Esther 4:16
[2] Psalms 68:5
[3] Proverbs 21:1 NIV
[4] Psalm 146:7 NIV
[5] Psalm 75:6,7
[6] John 14:6
[7] John 10:10

Trapped: Finding the Way Out

[1] 2 Kings 5:14
[2] *The Sayings of Queen Elizabeth* by Frederick Chamberlin (London: John Lane, Bodley Head, 1923).
[3] *Steps Along The Way* (Denville, NJ: Dimension Books, 1976).
[4] *Jesus Is Victor* (Old Tappan, NJ: Fleming H. Revell Company/Chosen Books, 1985).

Fear: The Big Bear

[1] 1 John 4:18
[2] Ephesians 4:27 NIV
[3] James 4:7

Death and Grief: You Don't Stop Loving

[1] *The Poetical Works* (1970), "When I Am Dead, My Dearest" (1962).
[2] *This Is That.*

Seven — Physical Threads

Appearance: Confidence Conveyed

[1] 1 Timothy 2:9,10
[2] Letter to her husband, John Adams, May 1, 1780; from *Familiar Quotations* by John Bartlett.
[3] *Chanel,* by Edmonde Charles-Roux (New York: Alfred A. Knopf, 1975).
[4] *The Book of Household Management* (New York: Farrar, Straus and Giroux, 1969).
[5] *Out of the Saltshaker and Into the World* (Downers Grove, IL: InterVarsity Press, 1979).

Exercise: Revitalize Your Well-Being

Graceful Growth: From Youth to Maturity

[1] Galatians 5:22,23
[2] Ephesians 5:26
[3] Romans 12:2
[4] 1 Peter 5:7
[5] Philippians 4:8
[6] 2 Corinthians 10:5 NAS
[7] *The Best Loved Poems of the American People,* edited by Hazel Felleman (Garden City, NY: Doubleday & Co., 1936), "Up-Hill" (1861).

Graceful Growth: Becoming "More Mature"

[1] Luke 12:6 NIV
[2] *The Unique Woman* (Tulsa: Honor Books, 1989).
[3] *The Unique Woman.*
[4] *Disciplines of the Heart* (Dallas, TX: Word Books, 1987).
[5] *Final Harvest* (Boston: Little, Brown and Company, 1961).
[6] *The Autobiography of Eleanor Roosevelt* (New York: Harper and Brothers, 1961).

A Final Word

[1] 2 Corinthians 5:17
[2] 1 John 1:9

For more information about Edwin and Nancy Cole's ministry to men, write: Christian Men's Network International Headquarters
P. O. Box 610588 • Dallas, Texas 75261

Also by Nancy Corbett Cole (and Edwin Louis Cole): *The Unique Woman*